WORD
BIBLICAL
THEMES

WORD
BIBLICAL
THEMES

Philippians

GERALD F. HAWTHORNE

WORD BOOKS
PUBLISHER
WACO, TEXAS

A DIVISION OF
WORD, INCORPORATED

PHILIPPIANS
Word Biblical Themes

Quotations from the holy Scriptures in this volume are the author's own translation from original languages unless otherwise identified. Those indicated PHILLIPS are from *The New Testament in Modern English, Revised*, by J. B. Phillips, published by The Macmillan Company, © 1958, 1960, 1972 by J. B. Phillips. Scriptures indicated NEB are from *The New English Bible*, © The Delegates of The Oxford University Press and the Syndics of The Cambridge University Press, 1961, 1970.

Library of Congress Cataloging-in-Publication Data

Hawthorne, Gerald F., 1925–
  Philippians.

  (Word Biblical themes)
  Bibliography: p.
  Includes index.
  1. Bible. N.T. Philippians—Criticism,
interpretaion, etc. I. Title. II. Series.
BS2705.2.H39 1987   227'.606   87-8171
ISBN 0-8499-0580-X   pap. 0-8499-3081-2

Printed in the United States of America
7898 RRD 987654321

To all my friends at
Bethany Chapel, Wheaton
Ho theos eulogoiē pantas hymōn

CONTENTS

FOREWORD

It is a distinct pleasure to introduce Gerald Hawthorne's study of theological themes from *Philippians*. Conceived as a companion book to the author's larger and more technical commentary on the epistle in the *Word Biblical Commentary* series, it builds—as one might expect—on a solid foundation of careful and comprehensive exegetical work. Yet it is no mere precis or reworking of the earlier commentary.

That commentary which has received a bevy of laudatory and appreciative reviews was designed to appeal to the scholar, the student, and the seminarian in the classroom. Here is a valuable distillation of the chief themes of Paul's joyful letter. It is designed for the busy pastor, the Sunday school teacher, and the layperson who wants an overview, in personal and practical terms and expressed in understandable language, of what this letter says to today's church and world.

Dr. Hawthorne is to be congratulated on achieving a fine balance. The exegetical discussions are largely taken for granted—and interested readers may go back to the *Commentary* for details; the applications of Paul's letter are clear and pertinent. Many a sermon will surely be sparked by this volume in what, it is hoped, will be a continuing series.

Fuller Theological Seminary
Pasadena, California

Ralph P. Martin
New Testament Editor
Word Biblical Commentary

PREFACE

On the one hand, to be asked to do a study on the theological themes in Philippians is a very great honor, and I owe a debt of gratitude to Professor Ralph P. Martin for asking me to do this. On the other hand, to attempt to fulfill such a request is a humbling experience indeed. Who is capable of writing on such great themes as God, Christ, salvation, and so on?

When I began to bring together what Paul had to say in Philippians about God, plunging feverishly into the subject, I was arrested by the account of Stephen's sermon in the Book of Acts. In rehearsing Israel's history Stephen recounted how Moses saw a bush in flames without any signs of it being burned up, and how he brashly turned aside to examine it more closely (*katanoēsai*), until he heard a voice that caused him to tremble all over—a voice that said, "I am God. . . ," and, in effect, "Do you know where you are, or what you are doing?" (Acts 7:31, 32).

Of a sudden I realized that I was quite like Moses on the occasion of the burning bush—not fully understanding where I was or what I was doing. For I was eagerly studying Paul's remarks about God, as though by close observation it would be possible to understand, to apprehend *(katanoēsai)* God, and thus be able to express him adequately. I was shattered by this flash of insight concerning my foolishness, and was forced to apologize to the Almighty for such thoughtless arrogance. This "encounter" stopped all my endeavors to proceed with my work, until I read on in Stephen's sermon. The voice that caused Moses to tremble also commissioned him to trek on down to Egypt to do a work for God there. God is a gracious God, full of understanding, mercy, and forgiveness. He made me pause, to be sure, and to reflect, but then encouraged me to go on and finish.

I have done that now, not with any sense that all of the significant themes in Philippians have been dealt with, nor that those dealt with have been discussed adequately. But I send this volume on its way, confessing as I do so that I owe so much to so many people whose works I have read, and whose ideas have shaped my thinking. I am deeply grateful to each and every one, although they are too many to name. Most of these, however, have been identified in a larger work on Philippians that I had the privilege of writing (*Philippians*, Word Biblical Commentary, vol. 43, Word Books, 1983), and that book may be consulted for a full bibliography should one wish to have this information in hand.

I am also grateful to Jane and Lynn, and to Jack Levison, who helped me view these themes from different perspectives, and who forced me to express my ideas more clearly. Especially do I owe a debt of love to Bill and Judy Pollard, who, by honoring us in an ineffable way, gave us courage to continue to study, to think, and to write.

Gerald F. Hawthorne
Wheaton (Ill.) College

INTRODUCTION

Philippi and the beginning of the church

This letter that bears the name, "To the Philippians," was addressed to the church in Philippi. Philippi was then an important city in northeast Greece (Macedonia). The emperor Octavian made it a Roman colony, and gave to its citizens the rights and privileges of those born and living in Rome. According to the account in Acts the church in Philippi began in a small way: Paul, on his second missionary journey, left Asia Minor for Macedonia, came to Philippi, went outside the city to the riverside, found a Jewish place of prayer, preached the gospel, and Lydia, a prominent woman from that area, and a few others became Christians. The church apparently was first housed in Lydia's home (Acts 16:9-40). In spite of its small beginnings, it nevertheless grew and became an active Christian community, taking an important part in evangelism (Phil 1:3-8), readily sharing its own material possessions (4:16), and generously sending one of its own people to assist Paul in his work and aid him while he was in prison (2:25-30). Paul visited this church on at least three different occasions (Acts 16:12, his initial visit, and Acts 20:1-6, which refers to his two later visits; cf. also 2 Cor. 2:13) and found it to be an increasing delight to him (Phil 4:1).

Author, place, and date

No writer in ancient times and scarcely any today questions that Paul wrote the letter to the Philippians. But from where did he write it, and when? And is it one letter or several? On these questions there is a great divergence of opinion. Most scholars assume that Paul wrote Philippians from Rome. Others have suggested Corinth and Ephesus. A good case can also be made for Caesarea. But wherever Paul was when he wrote, it had to be a place where he was in prison, where there was a Roman praetorium (i.e. the emperor's palace, or any provincial governor's official residence, 1:12, 13)*, and where there were members of Caesar's household (i.e. the royal entourage at the palace or the staff at a provincial capital, cf. 1:12, 13; 4:22). Hence, Rome (*ca.* A.D. 60), or Caesarea (*ca.* A.D. 58) are the cities frequently suggested as the most likely places, since each had a praetorium with its entourage, and in each Paul was known to have been jailed.

Unity of the letter

An increasing number of scholars are agreed in seeing Philippians not as a single letter, but as several woven into one—at least two, possibly three. The disjointed nature of the letter as it stands (cf. the abrupt transition in tone and

---

* Throughout this volume when reference is made to chapter and verse, it is the book of Philippians that is referred to unless identified otherwise.

content between 3:1 and 3:2); Paul's leaving his "thank you" to the end (4:10-20); and Polycarp's reference in his own letter to the Philippians to Paul's having written them several letters (Pol. *Phil.* 3:2), are some of the reasons given for suggesting the possibility that Philippians is a composite writing made up of different letters, or letter-fragments, sent to Philippi, and then welded together into the single letter that is known today. But for other scholars the abruptness noted above is hardly an argument against the integrity of Philippians, for the letter's style and structure are not inconsistent with the characteristics of private speech, nor out of line with Paul's style of writing noted elsewhere (cf. Rom 16:16-18; 1 Thess 2:13-16). And although Polycarp says that Paul wrote several letters, he apparently knew and used no other than this one.

Paul's opponents

Because of who Paul was, a self-proclaimed apostle, "the least" of them, "not worthy to be called an apostle," a former persecutor of the church of God (1 Cor 15:9), and because of how he lived as a Christian, that is to say, aggressively for the gospel (cf. 1 Cor 15:10), all out for Jesus Christ (Phil 3:4-11), he seemed to attract hostility both to himself and to his message. So it is not surprising to learn that, when he wrote his letter to the Philippians, there were at least two groups of people who opposed him. One was a group of Christians who were jealous of him, and who, while he was in prison, preached Christ more openly, thinking to make his life as a prisoner more difficult (1:15-17).

The other was a group of people who preached a gospel Paul would in no way identify himself with, and which, elsewhere, he called no gospel at all (cf. Gal 1:7).

It is not possible to precisely identify this latter group. (1) Some have suggested it was made up of Judaizers—Jewish

Christians who taught that in addition to believing in Christ one must also keep the Jewish law, including regulations about food and drink and especially the command concerning circumcision. (2) Others have said that this group was composed of those Judaizers who were influenced by gnosticism and thus who claimed to possess a "super-knowledge" that made them perfect and gave them liberty to do whatever they wanted to do with their bodies. (3) Still others see this group as comprising evangelistic Jews, not Christians in any way, whose programs of expansion conflicted with those of the apostle.

Whoever they were or whatever they taught may be questions that cannot be answered satisfactorily. But the presence and influence of these people dictated Paul's arguments in chapter 3: circumcision is worthless, personal pedigree is worthless, human achievement is worthless—all are worthless as far as establishing a right relationship with God is concerned. Only Christ can do this, and Christ has in fact already done it. Thus Christ is everything. Knowledge of and faith in Christ are essential for salvation, and pressing on to know Christ is the all-important endeavor of life.

Paul's reasons for writing Philippians

Paul's reasons for writing to his Christian friends at Philippi were many. He wanted above everything else to convey his continuing deep affection for them all (cf. 1:3-8). He wanted to bring them up-to-date on the news about himself (1:12-16; 2:24), to inform them of the erroneous but seductive teachings of the opponents of the true gospel (3:2-21), and to encourage them to stand firm for the faith (1:27-30).

He also wanted to inform them about Epaphroditus, their own messenger to him, and tell them how Epaphroditus had risked his life to carry out their orders and to fulfill the work of Christ in their behalf (2:25-30). He wrote them to correct division within their ranks (1:27; 2:2-4; 4:2), to exhort them to rejoice irrespective of circumstances (2:18; 3:1; 4:4), and to express his thanks for the gift of money that they sent to ameliorate his situation in prison. Philippians bears all the characteristics of a very personal letter, where the reasons for writing are various and numerous. It is like a chat, the subject matter changing without notice as in an informal conversation between friends. There seems, thus, to be no clear, identifiable, single reason for the existence of this letter, but many.

Paul and his encounter with Christ

Paul, as he himself says, was brought up in a traditional Jewish home which rigidly kept to Jewish beliefs and customs (3:5). Although he was born in Tarsus (Acts 22:3), the capital of the Roman province of Cilicia and the seat of a famous Stoic philosophical school, he was taken away from there as a child and sent to Jerusalem, the holy city of his people, to attend the school of the rabbis, before the pagan world could gain possession of his affections (Stauffer).[1] Thus it is quite likely that the background for Paul's thinking was not primarily Greek philosophy or Greek mystery religions as some have supposed, but Judaism, the teaching of the rabbinic schools, and especially those in Palestine.

In Jerusalem, under Gamaliel, the great Jewish rabbi, who was "held in esteem by all the people" (Acts 5:34), who was the grandson of Hillel, Paul was thoroughly trained in the intricacies of the holy law of God (Acts 22:3). He joined the order of strict observance of that law, the Pharisaic order (cf. Phil 3:5, 6), earned the confidence of his superiors, and was moving toward a promising career as a brilliant teacher of the law of God—all this, until a crisis event occurred in his life that totally revolutionized his thinking and altered his conduct, turning him around to proceed in precisely the opposite direction to that in which he had been headed.

According to the account in Acts, while Paul was on a mission to Damascus to stamp out the followers of Jesus, to rid the world of those who belonged to the Way, men or women, "to destroy the church of God" (cf. Gal 1:13), he was confronted by the resurrected and living Jesus—the very Jesus whose followers he was harassing (Acts 9:1-6; 22:3-8; 26:4-16). As a result the whole course of his life was changed. Paul, who formerly persecuted the followers of Jesus, became one himself and began now to preach the faith he once had tried to destroy (Gal 1:23).

There is not the slightest hint, either in Luke's account of Paul's life (Acts), nor in his own autobiographical remarks to indicate that Paul was unhappy with his career, dissatisfied with or skeptical about his beliefs, or psychologically disturbed about anything he was doing—neither about his attacks on Jewish Christians nor about the stoning death of Stephen (cf. Acts 7:59-8:1a; 9:1, 2). Thus no natural explanation can account for his dramatic conversion experience. Paul appears to have been convinced that he was on a divine mission, fortified with an inner assurance that what he was doing was right and good, that even his brutal activity was a zeal for God (cf. Rom 10:2), that his putting "bad" Jews—i.e. Jews who believed that Jesus was the Messiah—to death was a matter of offering up acceptable service to the Almighty (cf. John 16:2).

Hence, one can say with a degree of confidence that there was nothing within Paul himself that triggered such a radical change in his life. Rather, as he himself said, it was something—more precisely, Someone outside him that brought about the change. It was a face-to-face meeting with Jesus. It was no vision merely, if his own testimony is to be believed, but a genuine encounter with the crucified, resurrected, living, challenging Jesus, whose real existence Paul could now no longer deny (Gal 1:15-16; 1 Cor 9:1; 1 Cor 15:7-9;

cf. Acts 9:1–6; 22:3–10; 26:9–18). It was this spectacular meeting that transformed him from a persecutor of Jesus into Jesus' most devoted and loyal follower.

The effects of this personal encounter with Christ never wore off or wore thin. When Paul wrote to the Philippians many years after the Damascus experience, he still stressed the overwhelming and life-altering importance of Christ. It is clear from what he wrote them that he had no regrets about having given up everything he had achieved before for Christ's sake. He had no reservations either about urging others to follow his example (Phil 3:7, 8, 17). Paul was obsessed with Christ, because for him Christ was everything he had been searching for in life and more.

Themes in Philippians

Philippians is an intensely intimate and personal letter. The church at Philippi, founded by Paul, was deep in his affections (1:7). For this reason he felt secure in revealing so much about himself (3:4–11), and expressing his anxious concern for their problems (2:1–4; 3:17–19; 4:2–4). This is a letter that deals with many of the ups and downs that go to make up common, everyday life. It is in no way a tract on theology. And yet the themes that run throughout Philippians are theological. Paul thinks theologically and he cannot write even about the most mundane aspects of existence—a quarrel in the church, illness in the family, and so on—without writing about God or Christ, or what God has done in Christ.

The purpose of this present volume, then, is to sort through Paul's letter to the Philippians and bring together in one place, into some kind of order, the various theological themes that are scattered everywhere throughout the letter. It is certainly the hope of the present writer that, in the process of taking this venture, what is vital will not become sterile, what is woven into the very fabric of life will not become unraveled or lose any of its beauty, and what is easily understood because of its living context will not become abstract and incomprehensible because it has been extracted from the context and systematized. Rather, it is hoped that just the reverse of this will be the result of such an effort.

Not all the themes that will be discussed here are necessarily unique to Philippians. But they are nevertheless expressed in a unique way because of the particular situation in which the Christians at Philippi found themselves. The themes to which special attention will be drawn here are: (1) God, his distinctiveness, his sovereignty, and his activity in history; (2) the providence of God and the problem of evil; (3) Christ, his special place in Paul's thinking as this is expressed by the titles he uses to describe him, and (4) by his composition of a hymn about Christ—a hymn that *is* unique to Philippians; (5) salvation, what it is and how it is achieved; (6) the Christian life, giving special attention to what characterizes it, and by what power it can be lived; and finally, (7) joy. This theme is not found only in Philippians, but certainly because it radiates through every part of the letter and because the words "joy" and "to rejoice" are found more times in this letter than in any other of Paul's letters, or many of them together, it is proper to say something about it in this volume.

Inasmuch as it is possible to do so, the attempt here is to codify Paul's thought about each of these subjects without reading into the text something the apostle never said or intended. It is Paul's thinking on each of these topics that is important. And yet it has been the position of the church that divine inspiration filled this author, and that while the thoughts expressed in the letter to the Philippians were indeed the thoughts of Paul, they were at the same time the thoughts of God. This, then, is all the more reason to make certain that ideas are not read into the text which were not there at all by someone who now wishes to put these thoughts in an ordered form.

1   THE CHARACTER OF GOD

Philippians is a letter written by a man to his friends, and not a treatise on theology. And yet what is striking about this letter is the many times the word God (*theos*) is used within its brief compass—twenty-four times to be exact! Certainly God was not at the periphery of Paul's thinking, but at the center. So, although it is a letter and not a theological tract, it is possible to learn from it a considerable amount of information about Paul's theology, about his understanding of God and his attitude toward God. To be sure, not everything Paul believed about God is to be found here, but the following things can be learned.

Transcendence and distinctiveness

Paul uses throughout the Greek word *theos*—the term regularly used to translate the Hebrew words *'el*, *'eloah*, *'elōhim*—when he writes about God. From his Jewish background and training he would have included in this title the rich understanding of the Old Testament. For him, then,

God was the first and the last, the eternal, the Almighty, the Living One, Creator of heaven and earth and everything in them. God was master over the world and its kingdoms, transcendent Being, not dwelling in temples made by human hands, nor served by humans as though he needed anything. He is the one who exists in the light where no person can approach, exalted above time and space, unique, holy, all-wise, invisible, immortal, king of kings and Lord of Lords (Gen 1:1; 2:4; Exod 3:14; 20:3, 4; Lev 19:2; Ps 36:9; Isa 37:16; 40:25; 44:6; Hab 3:3; see also Rom 1:20-23; 11:36; 16:26, 27; 1 Cor 8:4-6; Gal 3:20; Col 1:15, 16; 1 Thess 1:9; cf. Acts 17:24, 25; Eph 4:6; 1 Tim 2:5; 6:15-18). This was God for Paul; and the Philippians who had been taught by Paul would have understood from this very word he used for God, *theos*, that God was indeed unique, set apart from all other beings, different from, wholly other than everything else—sole, supreme, sovereign. He was *theos*, the one before whom all should bow in awe and reverence.

Because of this uniqueness, it is God, and only God, that Paul calls "Father" (1:2; 2:11; 4:20; cf. 2:15). By the use of this new title, not unknown to Old Testament writers, he intended to convey to the Philippians, at the very least, the thought that God is progenitor, that is, he is the source of all existence—their existence (2:15), and that of all other created beings as well (2:11). As such he is the one to whom obedience is justly due (cf. Deut 14: 1-3).

Perhaps it is for this reason that Paul makes it clear to the Philippians that God is the one to whom people are ultimately to give their praise. All acts of every person, he implies, should be directed toward bringing glory to God, whether the good deeds of Christians (1:11), or the acknowledgement of all creatures that Jesus Christ is Lord (2:11). "To the glory and praise *of God*," is the refrain that repeats itself in this letter.

Paul also tells the Philippians that when they offer up

their sacrifices—not now the blood sacrifices of animals, but their generous gifts given to meet the needs of others—they are offering them to God, and this is the way it should be. These their offerings, then, that immediately benefit people, are in fact offerings that are made to God, are pleasing to God, and are accepted by God (4:18). Christians should understand, therefore, that it is God who ultimately deserves the gifts and sacrifices of human hearts and hands (cf. Rom 12:1,2).

Furthermore, when Paul writes to the Philippians explicitly about worship, that is, when he actually uses the verb "worship" (3:3), he makes it clear that it is God who is to be worshiped. To be sure, the best texts do not actually include the word "God" as the direct object of the verb here. But both the context and the special word that Paul uses for "worship" (*latreuō*) indicate that for him God is indeed its object and must be the object (cf. Exod 20:5; Deut 6:13; 10:12, 20; Matt 4:10; Rom 1:9)—"We worship God," he says (cf. TEV, RSV, Goodspeed, Phillips). In a guarded way he acknowledges that every knee will bow to Jesus as Lord (certainly to bow the knee is a gesture of worship, 2:10, 11). And he understands that some people worship God incorrectly (he implies that only Christians are capable of worshiping God in the right way, 3:2, 3), acknowledging that there are people who foolishly worship something other than God as God (3:19). But none of these qualifications takes away completely from the fact that for Paul God (*theos*) is finally the one to be worshiped.

Consequently when Paul comes to offer up his own doxology of worship, it is solely to God that he directs it: "Now surely the glory belongs to God our Father forever and ever. Amen!" (4:20). To God alone belongs the glory!

Paul was most certainly a Christian. There is no doubt but that Paul believed Christ was divine; and Paul's devotion to Christ was boundless (see chapter 3). But he is careful, nonetheless, to make a distinction between God and Christ, a distinction preserved throughout the letter to the Philippians. For example, the fruit of righteousness is produced *through* Jesus Christ, but it is *for* the glory of God (1:11). Christians are called "children of God" (2:15), but not children of Christ. Righteousness comes through faith in Christ, but its origin is from God (3:9). Only God is the object of prayer and thanksgiving and worship (1:3; 3:3; 4:6). Only God is called upon to bear witness (1:8), and so on. Thus for Paul, God, *theos*, is in a class by himself, distinct from all others as unique.

Immanence and activity

God may indeed be wholly other, supreme, sovereign, set apart from everything else, transcendent, unique. But it is clear from this letter that Paul does not therefore understand God as one who simply created the universe, including humankind and the world, and then proceeded to absent himself from this creation, allowing it to run along on its own, governed solely by the laws he established for it. Rather, Paul understands God as present within this world, actively sustaining it, interestedly governing its affairs, very much involved in it, and, more importantly, as one who is intimately and kindly involved in the affairs of the people in this world. He sees God as interested in the immediate and ultimate well-being of these special objects of his creative love and concern, drawing near them, intervening in their histories, giving them things to be thankful for, allowing them to experience pain and problems, setting the highest standards of expectations for them, and actively participating in their lives so that they might reach these expectations.

Notice how Paul gives expression to these ideas.

1. As strange as it may seem, in the light of the awesome majesty of God, Paul makes it clear that individual people,

people who believe in God, to be sure, can speak quite personally of him as *their* God. Twice over Paul encourages this understanding by his own use of the expression, "*my* God" (1:3; 4:19). God, then, is not so far removed as to be impersonal. He is in fact so near as to belong to his people. "My God," therefore, is not a word of arrogance, but the humble recognition that God has willingly entered into a close and intimate relationship with his people. "God is never so far off as even to be near/ our hearts are the homes he holds most dear. . . ."

2. Although Paul perceived God as separate from, above and beyond his creation, he was certain that God was at the same time continuously expressing himself within his creation, at work in the lives of the people he had made, revealing himself both in their individual and corporate histories. He leaves no doubt about this when he writes the Philippians, "God is at work in you creating both the desire and the drive to promote good will" (2:13).

The church at Philippi was composed of men and women, who, along with their good qualities, had many deficiencies—conceit, pride, selfishness, unconcern for others, harmful ambition, and so on—deficiencies that work destructively within the individual and within the congregation. Paul was concerned that the Philippians change their ways and begin to serve each other following Christ's example (2:1-11). He begged them to work at bringing about healing ("salvation") within their ranks, harmony among themselves, and concern for one another, and to keep at this supremely difficult task until it was finished. And he could encourage them like this—to get busy and do their part in restoring harmony to their divided community, because he was confident that they were not on their own in striving to solve their problems. He was certain that God was already doing his part, already at work within them to help them bring to reality the very thing desired of them and by them.

The Character of God

3. Paul makes still more clear his belief that God, though transcendent in character, is actively at work in human history when he recounts his experience with Epaphroditus (2:25-30; 4:18). The Philippian church had sent to Paul this extraordinary man. He brought their gifts to Paul, making him rich; and Epaphroditus was himself their supreme gift, intended by them to be at hand to take care of the apostle's every need. He endeared himself to Paul, whom Paul called his "brother," "fellow worker," and "fellow soldier" (2:25).

But Epaphroditus fell ill. From Paul's perspective he most certainly would have died had not God intervened. Paul does not say what the nature of this sickness was, nor does he mention anything of his own prayers for Epaphroditus's recovery, or the laying on of hands, or the calling of the elders or the doctors, or the use of medicine—although all of these measures may have been employed. That of which Paul was overwhelmingly convinced, and to which he gives sole expression, is that God had stepped in and stopped the sickness. Paul perceived that the healing of his friend was a sovereign, merciful act of God himself. "God," he wrote, "took pity on him; not only on him but on me as well" (2:27).

4. Because God is not so far above this world that he has no contact with or concern for it, or cannot intervene in human affairs, prayer was for Paul a most meaningful endeavor. Hence, he was not at all hesitant to encourage his friends to pray, to bring to God in prayer all the things that made them anxious (4:6). When he told them that if they did so, the peace of God would guard their hearts and minds (4:7), he was not saying that God would automatically give his people precisely what they asked for when they asked for it. But he was saying still one more time that God is decidedly at work in the lives of human beings. He is actually present and operative to create within people a peace that will keep guard over their thoughts and feelings whether he

answers their prayers in precisely the way they had hoped for or not.

5. This same notion of God as sovereign, supreme, transcendent—who is nevertheless nearby, close to and involved in the histories of individual people and whole communities—gives Paul confidence to tell the Philippian church that God will meet and supply their every need out of his marvelous wealth in Christ Jesus (4:19). When Paul talks of their "needs" here, he does not have in mind their spiritual needs, or the needs that will be taken care of only when they reach heaven. The needs he has in mind are like those mentioned earlier in verse 16, namely, present material needs that can only be met by present, material resources.

And the God Paul knows is that supreme being who owns the material resources of this world and who is himself active within it to direct the dispensing of these resources. He will supply the needs of his people. It might be argued that the future indicative, "will supply," should not be taken literally, that is, as a precise statement of what God most certainly *will* do (who is a human being to say what God will do in a particular situation?). Might that statement be rather a prayer, expressing Paul's wish for what God will do for the Philippians—"In return for your meeting my needs, I pray that my God may meet all your needs." Nevertheless, it is a reiteration of Paul's conviction of what God *can* do, because God is present and operative within the world he has created (cf. 2 Cor 9:8).

6. God is holy and exalted above all—God most high. As such he has set the highest standards of expectation for his people. Paul speaks of the "upward call" (*anō klēseōs*) of God (3:14). The meaning of this expression evades precise explanation, but it may at least give the direction God has set for his people—upward, toward himself, toward goodness and life, not downward, tending toward evil and destruction. It is a call to come up to God.

The Character of God

Further, Paul calls attention to the "righteousness of God" (3:9). This is a term frequently used by Paul elsewhere and is explained by him in detail in other places (see Romans, Galatians). But used here it again tells the Philippians of a holy God's high expectations for his people. In essence, "the righteousness of God" is a call for human beings to be as right as God is right, to be as just and good as God, to measure up to God, to measure up to God's standard of moral perfection. And the call includes both expectation and demand.

If this is so, and if people fall short of such high expectations (as is clear from even a cursory reading of Philippians, cf. 1:15, 17; 2:2-4, 14; 4:2), and if all are thereby threatened with divine judgment because of this failure (cf. Rom 1:18), it was necessary for God to involve himself in human history in order to correct this fatal flaw, to rescue human beings from their predicament, to lift them up, and to make it possible for them to meet the divine demands placed upon them. And for Paul this is precisely what God did. When Paul wrote to the Philippians about the righteousness of God (3:19), he was not only speaking of a property that belongs to God—i.e. righteousness is something that belongs to God, God *is* righteous. He was also speaking of an action of God by which God provides for all people the very righteousness that is required, the kind of righteousness that will stand up in the day of testing. It is a righteousness that comes from God to erring people through faith in Jesus Christ.

More will be said about this in chapter 5, but for now it is sufficient to note that for Paul God is indeed the holy God, God most high, who has set the highest expectations conceivable for people to meet. But he is not so high and holy that he did not stoop to involve himself directly in human affairs, and most profoundly so in saving his people from destruction by providing them with the very righteousness he demanded from them. Thus God for Paul is Savior in the ultimate sense of this word (1:28).

7. Paul uses the Christ-hymn (2:6-11) to show that although God transcends history, he nevertheless acts in history. He acts to exalt those who obey him, who humble themselves to serve others, who do not first seek their own benefit. Paul uses the hymn to teach the Philippians a fundamental lesson of life. Whereas they were acting in a spirit of ambition, thinking themselves better than others, believing they were above serving their fellows, and studying how they might promote themselves and get ahead, the Jesus of the hymn never once fought for his own honor and right and credit. Rather through self-surrender, self-renunciation and self-sacrifice he pursued the benefit of others. In doing this he obeyed God. So radical was his obedience to God, that he did not withdraw it even when he was faced with death.

As a result, so the hymn makes clear, God stepped into human history and exalted Jesus. It brings to expression the idea that God sees the actions of human beings, evaluates them, approves of some, stands opposed to others, and acts to reward people whose attitudes and actions accord with his own self-giving nature.

8. In a form characteristic of the letter-writing of his day Paul gives thanks to God (1:3). But for what? Most certainly he thanks God for the partnership of the Philippians with him, for their help in the gospel from early on until the time he wrote. He thanks God for their gifts, their time, their energy, their personal involvement in the business of proclaiming the good news that occupied all of his own time.

But a more careful reading of the text discloses that Paul saw God in all this good work of the Philippian Christians. Paul saw God as the real motivating force behind the scenes who was prompting them to action. And further, Paul was confident that God would continue this good activity within them, would never leave them alone, would never withdraw his power from them until the work he had begun within them was completed (1:3–6). Thus, not only does Paul thank God for what the Philippians were doing, but for what God himself was doing in them.

Behind any good action, then, Paul ultimately saw God at work, and for this he was deeply grateful. God, for him, was transcendent, wholly above and apart from his creation, and yet paradoxically he was immanent, present in it, busy carrying out his purposes, all of which were good.

2 THE PROVIDENCE OF GOD AND THE PROBLEM OF EVIL

It is clear from the survey in chapter 1 that for Paul God is not only transcendent—the Being above, and independent of the worlds he created—but also immanent, the Being present within these worlds, the one who sustains them, governs their movements, and especially cares for, plans for, and provides for his people.

In theological language this is called the providence of God. Although Paul never used this term, he affirmed its meaning. When one today talks about the providence of God, that person has in mind the detailed providing care of a personal God, the painstaking, watchful, attentive supervision of this God over his creatures—especially over those creatures made in his own image and likeness—and the affection he has for them which prompts him to act in their behalf and to provide for them in their neediness.

This is a marvelous concept which can rather easily be affirmed when everything in life goes well, such as when sick people recover their health (cf. 2:25-30), when nice things happen to individuals. One can also rather easily say that back behind every good action God is there, already at work, ultimately responsible for bringing that good act into existence.

Posing the problem

But what happens to one's concept of the providence of God when things do not turn out as one had hoped? What becomes of one's belief in the benevolent providing care of God when bad things happen to good people?

It is only too painfully obvious from personal experience that life, even that of the person of faith, is often hurt-filled, sorrow-filled, and crushing. There is indeed about life in this world an ambiguity. It can be characterized as made up of events pleasant and unpleasant, of things good and bad, of triumphs and tragedies. And to some it would appear that the unpleasant, the bad, the tragedies outweigh the pleasant, the good, and the triumphs. Where is the sovereign God of whom it is claimed that he acts to intervene in human history in all of this sadness? Where is evidence of the detailed provident care of a personal God?

Here, of course, one comes up against the age-old problem of evil: How can a person continue to believe in a God who is all-knowing, all-powerful, absolutely good, both transcendent and immanent, above this world and actively present in it, who provides for his people's needs, and at the same time acknowledge the ubiquitous presence of pain? How can a person continue to assert that this God really intervenes in human history, and at the same time be aware that evil and not good seems to be on the throne?

What Paul wrote to his friends at Philippi throws some light into the darkness of this difficult question. It is necessary to keep in mind, however, that Paul was writing a letter, and not a tract. He was not consciously giving an answer to people who were directly asking questions about the problem of evil in light of the providence of God. Nevertheless, what he says about this troublesome problem just in passing is worth noting and reflecting upon.

It must be remembered that Paul was thoroughly convinced that God exists, that he is sovereign, that he is all-powerful and that he is transcendent over his creation. Paul was equally convinced that God is at the same time actively at work within his creation, that he is good, even ultimate goodness, the source of all grace, mercy, and favor (1:2), the God of peace, wholeness, health, soundness (4:7), who acts in history to bring healing, wellness, and salvation (1:28; 2:12–13).

Further, this conviction about God that Paul held to so tenaciously was not in the least shaken by his having at the same time to acknowledge the fact that this world was no paradise. He readily admitted the reality of sickness and the pain that sickness can cause, not only to the one afflicted but to that person's family and friends (2:26, 27). He was quite aware of the devastating possibility of death and the suffering it can bring (2:27).

Paul knew from personal experience that professing Christians, "brothers" (1:14), can do good things with bad motives, that those whom he might have expected to be with him turned out to be against him, that those he had hoped would help him were intent on hurting him, stirring up more trouble for him while he was in prison (1:15–17).

He was quite aware that even within a select community—the church—people nevertheless could and did act out of selfish ambition, party spirit, conceit, arrogance, self-interest (2:3, 21); that they could and did fight with each other, creating disunity and disharmony, displaying a divided front against a concentrated enemy (1:27b; 2:2; 4:2). He acknowledged the fact that good people suffer, even suffer while doing good or even because they are doing good (1:28, 29). The ultimate example of which, Paul says, is Jesus himself (2:6–8).

And yet, without once glossing over the evil that exists in the world, or failing to recognize its presence at every turn, Paul nevertheless never weakens in his firm belief that God is sovereign and good and at work in this world to bring about goodness and wellness and wholeness. He is able to hold these two ideas together with equal conviction for the following reasons.

Attempts to solve the problem

1. Paul seems ready enough to grant that there is mystery in the operation of providence. From his perspective God does not universally work in ways that either he (Paul) or his friends could explain or would have planned or chosen for themselves (2:26, 27a; cf. 2 Cor 12:7–10). Yet experience taught him that God was guiding and blessing even though the manner of that guidance and blessing could not readily be discerned or understood.

2. The many imperatives Paul uses in this letter imply he believed the providence of God takes into account human freedom—the freedom to make choices, whether good or bad, the freedom to decide on a course of action that could become the immediate cause of suffering and pain. The imperative mood is in effect an appeal of will to will. And without the power or authority to force one's will on another, any given command, no matter how good it is, may go unfulfilled simply because the person advised has chosen to ignore the advice. Hence, for Paul, providence works in people's choices, among them, with them.

If Paul's commands to be unselfish, charitable, interested in the welfare of others, and so on, are ignored by the Philippians—if they make bad choices as a result of failing to follow his wishes, or do evil things as a result of rejecting his orders—all is not lost. Even these bad choices and evil acts are somehow incorporated into the providential working of God (2:12, 13; cf. Gen 45:8).

3. There is implicit within Paul's remarks to the Philippians the idea that although God is not in a hurry, he nevertheless is relentless in carrying out his plan to overcome dissolution, frustration, and destruction. He is inexorably acting to save and make whole (1:28; 2:13), to transform and make beautiful (3:21), to provide the context in which all will openly acknowledge the one he has exalted and made Lord (2:11), and thus submit to his rule which is a rule of righteousness, justice, and goodness.

4. In thinking more deeply about so-called bad actions and the providence of God the apostle becomes so bold as to say that the suffering of good people is permitted by God. Being even more radical, Paul tells the Philippians that the suffering they had experienced while doing good, their suffering for Christ, was in fact a gift given them by God (1:29). To be sure, the literal translation of 1:29 is, "it has been granted to you on behalf of Christ to suffer for him," which, because of the use of the passive voice, could be construed to mean that God had nothing to do with their suffering at all. But the passive verb, "has been granted," is what is called a "divine passive." In such instances the passive statement can legitimately be transformed into an active statement that has God as its subject (Jeremias).[1]

Such a use of the passive voice here is but one more indication of Paul's firm conviction that:

> God is in control of all events. Therefore, the Philippians should not be upset by their bitter experience as if God had forgotten them or were angry with them. On the contrary, the verb . . . would remind them that even this trial comes to them as a gift of his grace. (Martin)[2]

This is made very clear from the word Paul uses here for "give." It is one of his special verbs formed from the same root as the word "grace." It conveys the idea of the free, unmerited favor or kindness of God (cf. Eph 4:32). It describes privilege—an idea that is reflected in some of the recent translations: "You have graciously been given the privilege of suffering for Christ" (cf. TEV, NEB, JB, Phillips).

Hence, the suffering of good people and the sovereignty of a good God were never viewed by Paul as mutually exclusive—"if one, then not the other." In this world created and controlled by God even the evil that people do, the wicked choices they make that work harm to others, can be traced ultimately to the door of one who is not only the all-mighty, but the all-good. Paul wrote out of faith and hope, to be sure. His, however, was not an infantile belief that the universe ought to be ordered to fit in with one's own ego-centered desires and ambitions. Providence for him was not just a belief in divine favors or a belief that everything must turn out well in the end. It was a belief in an ordering of history by a God who is holy and righteous as well as merciful (Macquarrie).[3]

5. From personal experience Paul became convinced and made it clear to the Philippians that a benevolent providence, which allows for and incorporates the free choices of people—many of those being evil choices—nevertheless produces good out of ill. It is not generally considered a good thing for a person to be thrown into prison. And if it is a bad thing now, it was even worse in Paul's day when the physical conditions of prisons were terrible and the treatment of prisoners brutal.

Yet although the apostle was a prisoner then, and was so not for wrong things he had done, but for good things, he nevertheless did not become bitter or resentful when he thought about his situation. Why? Because he saw God at work in all these painful events that had happened to him.

Instead of lamenting the ill that he was experiencing, he was happy for it, because he was confident that God was using it as a catalyst to encourage more and more Christians to become bold in speaking the gospel publicly. As a consequence, the very thing that Paul was most concerned to achieve—the rapid advance of God's good news (1:12-14)—but did not know precisely how to bring to reality was achieved. Many people long silent began to preach the gospel openly when they heard that Paul was in prison—some because they loved him deeply and wanted to do what he could not now do, others because they hated him and out of envy wanted to hurt him still more. Even those things that rightfully could be termed "evil" were made to serve a good purpose.

In reflecting on this experience Paul would not say that the envy and rivalry that motivated certain of these to preach the gospel were positive or constructive virtues. Nor was he applauding those who, because of selfish ambition sought to enhance themselves at his expense (cf. Gal 5:19-21). But he would say and did say that these negative, destructive attitudes and actions could not keep good from coming to expression. In fact, he went so far as to say, at least in this one instance, that good came to expression precisely because of such bad, negative, destructive attitudes and actions—that is, people were incited to preach the gospel (the good), because they were jealous of Paul (the bad), 1:15-18.

Thus, a person who is evil cannot take comfort from his evil, for he cannot be confident that the evil he plans and effects ever has the power to overcome the good. Why? Paul would answer: "Because God is at work in the world to turn the tables."

Although God permits, even defends, the freedom of people to choose what they want to be and do, he nevertheless delights to turn their most terrible choices around in such a way as to make these choices productive of the very best possible results. Did not Paul affirm elsewhere, while reflecting on the things that in themselves had the power to break people down—death, life, angels, demons, trouble, hardship, persecution, famine, nakedness, danger, sword—that God loves his people? Did he not assert that God is for them, that he stands with them in the middle of these threatening things, that he is actually working these all together for good for their benefit, that in everything they are conquerors, even more than conquerors (Rom 8:28–38)?

Like Paul, then, people of faith do not naively deny or brush aside as minuscule matters those events that do in fact ride over them, hurt them, and bring them down to the grave. The person of faith has the capacity to see beyond these would-be destructive forces to God who is above them, who is stronger than they, and who is using the things to work good in that person's life. Paul's word stands strong:

> In all these things we are more than conquerors,
> because of God who loves us. (Rom 8:37)

In all these things! Although Paul may not have been able to explain it, yet he believed that God can and does create good, not *apart* from the evil events that happen, but *in* them.

6. Finally, Paul is not afraid to say that the final resolution to the problem of evil lies outside of this world, beyond time, on the other side of the grave, but not apart from or outside of the providential care of God. Once again, we turn to the Christ-hymn (2:6–11). Here Jesus is presented as a good person committed to doing good. Jesus did not consider his own interests first. He was not selfish. He was not filled with vain conceit. He was not greedy or grasping. On the contrary he lived unselfishly. He poured himself out for others. He took a humble place and set himself to serve. Yet, paradoxically, those he aided put him

to death. Those he served killed him. Those he helped crucified him. Good was rewarded with evil. Evil triumphed. Is this so?

People without the faith-perception will invariably interpret life's events in precisely this way—evil on the throne; good on the cross. Hence, for them there is no advantage to being or doing good.

To the person of faith, however, the crucifixion of Jesus was not the triumph of evil over good; it was exactly the reverse of this. *But* this final triumph did not take place in time. Rather it took place beyond time, beyond death, beyond the grave. Paul is saying, in effect, that many of the most perplexing problems of suffering in this world—many, if not most, of the troublesome questions that arise because of pain—can only be resolved in the resurrection life. The experience of Jesus, therefore, becomes a paradigm of hope for people who suffer and for all who ponder the suffering of others.

The Providence of God and the Problem of Evil

3   THE PERSON OF CHRIST

For the most part Paul's letters are not systematic presentations of his thinking. What is true of his letters in general is especially true of this letter to the Philippians. As I have said already, it is an intensely intimate and personal letter, dealing primarily with matters that involve Paul himself and his feelings, his friends and their problems. It cannot at all be considered a carefully worked out study in theology.

Yet Paul does indeed write theologically. Why? He does so because his mind is absolutely filled with thoughts of God, Christ, Spirit, the end-times, resurrection, the return of Christ, the new world—and more. Christ especially is at the center of his thinking, the driving force of his being. Hence, it is not surprising that Paul refers to Christ at least forty-seven times within the compass of this short letter. Christ was first, not only in the universe, and in the world (cf. Col 1:18), but also in Paul's own personal existence.

This preeminence of Christ pervades Philippians, but not in any formal way. Rather, the idea of Christ's centrality crops up everywhere, even in the most casual contexts, and in the most mundane comments. For every thought of the apostle, even the humblest, is affected by the power and presence of Christ. Nevertheless, for the purposes of this volume, an attempt will be made to gather up and systematize Paul's "random" remarks about Christ in his letter to the Philippians, and not leave them scattered about as they are. This can be done (1) by focusing attention on the titles Paul uses for Christ and later (2) by considering in detail the so-called Christ-hymn (2:6-11). In this chapter only the titles will be considered.

Jesus

Paul rarely refers in any of his letters to the person who transformed his life simply as "Jesus" (see Rom 3:26; 8:11; 1 Cor 12:3; 2 Cor 4:10-14; Gal 6:17; Eph 4:21; 1 Thess 1:10; 4:14), and never in Philippians (except at 2:10 in the Christ-hymn). This may be astonishing to those who are familiar with the Gospel tradition which says that "Jesus" was the name given to this special person in a special way by a special messenger to designate the special divine purpose of his life—"to save his people from their sins" (Matt 1:21).

Paul, however, was reluctant to use the name "Jesus," at least without some other descriptive title alongside it. Why was this? Perhaps it was because in Paul's day "Jesus" was such a common name that for the apostle it was not in itself capable of distinguishing him or setting him apart sufficiently from all other people (cf. Matt 27:16, in many Greek manuscripts). Or perhaps it was because for Paul "Jesus" was the name expressive merely of Christ's humanness. Certainly it was the name he bore from birth in Bethlehem, throughout his life on earth, up to and through his arrest, trial, and crucifixion (cf. Matt 1:21; Mark 1:9, 14; 14:53; 15:1, 37, 43; passim). And although Paul does indeed use this name in contexts of Jesus' resurrection and exaltation (Rom

8:11a; Phil 2:10; 1 Thess 4:14), yet it may have been that for him "Jesus" was the name which belonged primarily to the days of his humanity.

Paul seems thus to have preferred, or felt the need for, some other designation by which to say clearly that this Jesus who was crucified was more than a man. Recall the apostle's own words in 2 Corinthians 5:16:

> Even though we once regarded Christ from a human point of view (that is to say, though we humans could only judge Jesus from all outward appearances to be no more than a humble suffering human), yet we regard him thus no longer (that is, from the perspective of experience and revelation we now know that he was more than a mere human, more than the name "Jesus" has the capacity to connote).

In any case, it is true that the name "Jesus" figures hardly at all in this letter to the Philippians as a name for the most important figure in Paul's thought and life. And if he did use it in Philippians 2:10, he did not do so with the intention of saying, as some have suggested, that "Jesus" was *the* name Christians were to venerate above all other names. The expression, "at the name of Jesus," that occurs here (2:10) does not mean that everyone will bow before the name "Jesus." Rather it means that everyone will bow before the name Jesus bears, that is to say, before the new name Jesus is given, i.e. "Lord" (a fuller discussion comes later in this chapter).

Christ

In Philippians Paul uses the designation "Christ" by itself more frequently than any other designation, when he refers to this most important person of his life (1:10, 13, 15, 17, 18,

20, 23, 27, 29; 2:1, 16, 30; 3:7, 8, 9, 18). He uses it both with and without the definite article—"Christ"/"the Christ"—with apparently no difference in meaning. He uses it without explanation, without any indication of its importance, without a word of its long history of meaning. And yet certainly his mind must have been full of its rich significance.

The English word "Christ" is essentially a transliteration of the Greek word *Christos*. Paul did not coin this word, for it was used in the Greek Bible, the Septuagint, to translate the Hebrew *māšîach*, "messiah." So in using this designation, "Christ," Paul was simply borrowing an ancient word and concept to describe Jesus.

Both words—Christ and Messiah—mean "anointed one," or "the anointed one," and in general they referred to persons who were selected out and equipped by God to undertake and accomplish special tasks, and who were thus dependent upon and responsible to God (cf. 1 Sam 16:1-3).

In the Old Testament "messiah" was a title given to patriarchs (1 Chron 16:22; Ps 105:12-15), to priests (Lev 4:3, 5, 16), even to a pagan ruler (Isa 45:1), to Israelite kings (1 Sam 10:1; 24:6), and more particularly to David as king, and to his descendants (2 Sam 22:51; Ps 89:35, 36). The dominant messianic idea of the Old Testament that developed was thus one that centered in or revolved about the king of God's choosing, who was invested with authority, honor, and glory by means of the act of anointing with oil (cf. 1 Sam 16:1-3).

When the Davidic monarchy was being threatened and eventually overturned, there came the promise to the Israelites of a future king, himself a descendant of David, whose rule would be good and wise, secure and supreme (Isa 9:6, 7; 42:1-4; Ezek 34:23, 24; 37:24, 25). Setbacks and disappointments continued to mark the history of Israel and threatened to destroy their hope. Yet the people never surrendered to despair. Sometimes, it seems, the darker their history, the brighter the expectation of their deliverance shone (cf. 2 Apoc Bar 82–83). They fully anticipated the coming of a powerful king, the son of David, one permanently possessed of the Spirit of God, characterized by dignity and greatness (Isa 11:1, 2), who would shatter unrighteous rulers, purge Jerusalem from invading nations, destroy the pride of sinners, rebuke the godless, and lead the people in truth and goodness (Pss of Sol 17:21–38; 18:5–7). His kingdom would be a great and eternal kingdom of righteousness.

The preservation and persistence of this expectation of a coming king-deliverer can be traced on into later Judaism (2 Apoc Bar 70:8, 9; 4 Ezr 12:32; 4Q Flor 1:11), and into the New Testament (Matt 2:4–6; cf. Acts 1:6). To be sure, the expectation of Messiah as king was only one type of messianic expectation. On occasion messianic ideas were fashioned under the influence of thinking about the prophet-like-Moses who was to come (Deut 18:15–19), about Elijah (Sir. 48:10; cf. Mark 8:28), about the Son of Man (Dan 7:13), about the high priest (4Q Testim 14; 1QS 9:11). But the Davidic king-messiah was the principal or dominant messianic motif, nonetheless (2 Sam 7:13; Pss 89:3, 4, 28, 29; 132:11, 12; Isa 9:7; cf. Mic 4:7; Dan 7:14; 2 Bar 73).

What was different now in the New Testament was that for its writers the Messiah who was to come, the anointed of the Lord par excellence, had in fact come and could be named. He was Jesus (Luke 1:31–33; Mark 8:29; Luke 9:20; Matt 16:16; cf. Mark 15:26 par.).

For the whole of the New Testament, messianism no longer stands under the sign of expectation but under that of fulfillment. Everywhere the Christ event is spoken of in the perfect or past tense. The writings do indeed look into the future as well, sometimes very intensively. But the One who is awaited comes as the

One who has already come. He is not someone unknown; he is well-known to those who await him as
they are to him (cf. Jn 10:14). (Brown:Rengstorf)[1]

But that which was most strikingly new and different in
the New Testament, and probably the most difficult to accept, was that this long-expected Messiah who had come,
this longed-for bringer of salvation who had appeared,
turned out to be no powerful political figure. Rather, he was
a humble servant, no deliverer from Rome, but a savior from
sin. He was no marching king who would establish rule with
arms and armies, but the anointed of the Lord who would
show his strength by his weakness. The humbleness, weakness, suffering, and death of Jesus, then, did not discredit
him, or prove him to be a false Messiah, as most might have
inferred (cf. Acts 5:34-37); these were instead the very marks
of his messiahship, the means by which he acted as Messiah,
to save his people. But the proof that this was so, the evidence confirming that this "weak" Jesus was indeed the
anointed of God, was the resurrection. God identified Jesus
as his Messiah, his Christ, by raising him from the dead
(Mark 8:31, 32 pars; Acts 2:29-36; cf. Col 1:12, 13).

Surely all of this was in Paul's mind whenever he used
this word "Christ" in writing to the Philippians. And if
here in Philippians as in his other letters he seems to em-
ploy this title as little more than a name, it was because he
had already thoroughly explained to both his Jewish and
Gentile audiences the new meaning of this title. "Christ"/
"Messiah"—namely, the Son of David, the hope of Israel,
the Savior of the world (cf. Luke 2:10, 11)—was God's
suffering servant, Jesus (cf. Acts 17:1-3a; Isa 53). It was
possible for Paul to use "Christ" almost casually as a sobri-
quet—but one, nonetheless, with immense significance
both to himself and to his readers.

Thus in Philippians, as elsewhere in Paul's writings, the

apostle preferred to use "Christ" by itself without any other names or qualifiers, when he pointed his friends to *the* Deliverer, that supreme one who had accomplished the great work of salvation in their behalf. He wrote here such things as:

- "people preach Christ" (1:15–17)
- "Christ is preached" (1:18)
- "the gospel of Christ" (1:27)
- "the righteousness of God which is through faith in Christ" (3:9)
- "the cross of Christ" (3:18)

Each of these is a phrase pregnant with meaning. For to preach Christ, etc., was to proclaim that "Christ died for our sins" and was raised from the dead for our justification (1 Cor 15:3–5, 12–22; cf. Rom 4:5).

To Paul, Christ's death and resurrection, were those events that put sinners right with God, delivered them from this present evil world, transferred them from the kingdom of darkness into the realm of light, freed them from the power of evil, saved them from their sin, gave them life instead of death. To Paul "Christ" means deliverer, Messiah.

Paul came to understand all this as a result of his face-to-face meeting with the risen Christ. He may have listened carefully to the earliest Christians' message about Jesus; he may even have studied it carefully so as to know what was being said. But he bitterly opposed everything he had heard, until Jesus himself stopped him. From the moment of that encounter with Jesus onward Paul's life could only be summed up in one word—Christ. Christ and Christ alone now was the one who gave inspiration, direction, meaning, and purpose to his existence. Everything he did now could only be done for Christ. "Living is Christ," he wrote (Phil 1:21) meaning that his life was totally determined and controlled by his love for Christ.

The Person of Christ

Overpowered by Christ on the Damascus road and over-whelmed by his majesty and love and goodness and forgive-ness, Paul told the Philippians he could see no reason for existence except to be "for Christ" (1:21; cf. Rom 14:7-9). Thus it was that he committed himself to being the means by which Christ would become known, by which he would be made great in the eyes of all peoples (1:20).

For this reason also Paul gladly accepted such a radical transvaluation of values for himself, so that those things he once considered most worthwhile—birth, religion, position in society, and so on—he now considered worthless. He had come to understand that to gain everything and lose Christ was to profit not at all. But to lose everything, if need be, and gain Christ was to become the richest of the rich (3:7-10).

Christ Jesus/Jesus Christ

At least fifteen times within this letter to the Philippians Paul combines the two designations, "Jesus" and "Christ" (1:1, 6, 8, 11, 19, 26; 2:5, 21; 3:3, 12, 14; 4:7, 19, 21). Some may claim that it makes a difference to Paul in which order he places these names—i.e. when he wrote "Jesus Christ" he meant to direct attention to the man Jesus whom God raised up and to whom he accorded the dignity and position of the Christ, but when he wrote "Christ Jesus" he meant to direct attention to the preexistent Christ who revealed himself in a man, Jesus of Nazareth (Cerfaux).[2] But their claim cannot be established from Philippians alone. For one thing, the number of times this combination occurs here is too few. Fur-thermore, in eight of these occurrences the text is in question. Where some Greek manuscripts have "Christ Je-sus," others reverse the order and read "Jesus Christ."

The following, however, can be said with some degree of confidence: when Paul uses this double name he enhances the meaning of both by making clear who the Messiah/ Christ is: "The Messiah is Jesus," or "Jesus is the Christ."

There is no sufficient reason to say that when Paul coupled "Christ" with "Jesus" he gave it no more meaning than that found in a double name such as Caesar Augustus. Surely Paul himself, as has been noted above, understood the full significance of the word "Christ." He stood firmly "within the history of the living Messianic hope," but he had personally come to know the Messiah, whom the Jewish world around him did not know and still expected. He knew him to be Jesus of Nazareth.

Hence, to write "Jesus Christ" or "Christ Jesus" was for him a powerfully moving proclamation that the crucified one, the one he had fought against and persecuted, was indeed the Messiah, the hope of Israel, the Savior of the world (cf. 1 Cor 1:23, 24; 2:2). It can be imagined also that this truth was no less well understood by the Philippians, for the one who taught them was Paul himself, the Jew, the Pharisee, become Christian.

Thus in this combined name, "Jesus Christ"/"Christ Jesus" the Philippians, too, would have caught the significance contained in it, namely, that the longed for deliverer, the long-awaited Savior, the hope not only of ancient Israel, but of the new Israel, the Messiah, was Jesus. They too would have caught the sense of dignity and power and worth in the name "Jesus" when it was bound, as Paul bound it, so closely together with the title "Christ."

In this connection it is worth noting that the favorite expression of Paul, the one that is very important to him, but which he never fully explains—the expression "in Christ"—always appears in Philippians in the double form: never "in Christ" only but always "in *Christ Jesus.*"

In Christ Jesus the Philippians are called "holy ones, saints" (1:1; cf. 4:21); are to boast abundantly (1:26; 3:3); must govern their thinking and feeling (2:5); will find the peace of God guarding their hearts and minds (4:7); will have their every need met (4:19). The upward call of God is in Christ Jesus (3:14). Thus, like Paul, the Philippians, too, are to allow the whole of life to be determined by the fact of Christ Jesus. They stand before God *in* him.

Something of the profundity of this idea may be grasped when one makes the effort to understand that the early Christian writers perceived Christ Jesus not only as a single person in time and space, but also as a corporate person. Paul understood Adam to be an individual self and also a person who included all his descendants in himself, who in fact, embodied the whole world of human beings. Likewise, he understood Christ Jesus to be the Last Adam, the progenitor of a new race, a person who embodied all other persons in himself (see Rom 5:12-21; 1 Cor 15:22, 45-49; cf. Phil 1:1 [NEB]: "God's people incorporate in Christ Jesus").

> Paul had religious experiences in which Jesus of Nazareth . . . was found to be more than [an] individual. He was found to be an 'inclusive' personality. And this means, in effect, that Paul was led to conceive of Christ as any theist conceives of God: personal, indeed, but transcending the individual category. Christ is like the omnipresent deity "in whom we live and move and have our being." Jesus Christ . . . actually *is*, or constitutes that ideal society: He is the ultimate Adam, to be incorporated in whom is to belong to the renewed society. (Moule)[3]

Thus when Paul writes to the Christians at Philippi about being "in Christ Jesus" he is telling them, in effect, that as for him, so for them, "living means Christ" (1:21). Since they are incorporated into Christ Jesus, all that he is they are, and all that he has achieved they have achieved—Christ Jesus is their life and hope and joy, for God sees them in Christ Jesus, not as they are in and of themselves.

Lord

Paul uses the descriptive title "Lord" *(kyrios)* fifteen times in Philippians, and most frequently by itself, without any accompanying title or name—"rejoice in the Lord" (3:1), "the Lord is near" (4:5), and so on (see also 1:14; 2:24, 29; 4:1, 2, 4, 10). But he also uses it in combination with other words as well. He uses it with "Jesus"—"I hope in the Lord Jesus to send Timothy" (2:9), and with "Christ Jesus"/"Jesus Christ"—"Christ Jesus my Lord" (3:8; see also 1:2; 2:11; 3:20; 4:23). The fullest, most honorific title Paul uses of Jesus is "the Lord Jesus Christ" (1:2; 4:23).

The word "lord" *(kyrios)* comes from a root that means "having power," "competent," "decisive," "principal." The noun derived from this root identified a person as "lord," i.e. as the lawful owner of slaves and property, as the lord over subject peoples, the master of the house. As "lord" one could dispose of something or someone without consulting others, because he was the lawful owner of that person or thing.

From classical times "lord" *(kyrios)* was frequently used to refer to the gods, those with the legitimate power and right to control designated spheres. For example, Zeus was viewed as the Lord of all (Plato, *Laws* 12.13). "Lord" was employed also as a title of respect, especially when the person so addressed was a person of a higher rank than the one using it.

In the Septuagint, "lord" *(kyrios)* was also used to address people respectfully—"my lords" (Gen 19:2), or to refer to them as owners (Judg 19:22, 23), or masters (Gen 27:29, 37). But most frequently "Lord" was used here to translate the divine name, Yahweh, the name of God that described not only his sovereign power over all creation (cf. Ps 97:5; Mic

4:13; Zech 4:14; 6:5), but also the personal relationship in which he stood to his people (cf. Exod 15:1–3; Isa 64:12–65:5).

During the Roman period "lord" came to be used of the emperor. For instance, Caligula liked the title. Nero was described as "the Lord of the whole world." Domitian was hailed as "our Lord and God." Eventually to make the confession, "Caesar is Lord," became a sort of loyalty oath required of citizens in the Roman Empire.

When Paul wrote "Lord" in his letter to the Philippians he always ascribed the title to Jesus Christ—"Jesus Christ is Lord" (2:11; see also 1:2, 14; 2:19, 24, 29; 3:1, 8, 20; 4:1, 2, 4, 5, 10, 23). How did he come to use it in this way, and what did he mean by doing so?

Paul's reasons for saying "Jesus Christ is Lord"

The first question cannot be answered to everyone's satisfaction, for Paul himself does not precisely explain how he came to use the title "Lord" for Jesus. One can, however, offer suggestions based on what information is available. Perhaps Paul's strongest impulse to call Jesus Lord came from his own experience with Jesus (see the Introduction). This experience was so profoundly real that it transformed his life and revolutionized his thinking.

Paul understood now that God had raised Jesus from the dead, lifted him up above the limitations of space and time, and exalted him to a position no other human being held or had ever held. Paul's immediate response to Jesus was to obey everything he told him to do; it was as if Jesus now was the master and he the servant (cf. Acts 22:10). Thus, whoever wrote "the hour of Damascus is the key to Pauline theology" was quite right.

No person knows all that happened to Paul after his conversion and during his retreat to Arabia. But he himself discloses this much: He says that in Arabia (and Damascus) he received by divine revelation the gospel he was to preach, the gospel about Jesus Christ (Gal 1:1-17). Certainly while he was there he had time to reflect deeply on his encounter with Jesus and to square this experience with his knowledge of the Old Testament. And if his own growing inclination was to think of the risen Jesus as his Lord, he like others before him was able to find scriptural evidence for this in the Old Testament (cf. Ps 110:1: "The Lord says to my Lord: sit at my right hand until I make your enemies a footstool for your feet").

When Paul returned and began to enter into fellowship with Palestinian Christians he learned that they, too, from earliest times, had been calling Jesus Lord. Seemingly from the moment of the resurrection they were certain that God had exalted him to the position of universal Lord *(kyrios)*.

An indication of this can be found in what appears to be a very early Aramaic prayer—*Marana tha*, "Our Lord, come!" (1 Cor 16:22; cf. Rev 22:20), which, Paul writing to a Greek-speaking audience, quotes without translating. He did not need to translate it. Although it was originally formulated in Aramaic among the churches in Palestine, among Aramaic-speaking people, it had become a prayer familiar to all Christians everywhere hallowed through long usage in the liturgy—especially in that part of the liturgy pertaining to the communion Supper. There in the celebration of the eucharist Jesus was celebrated as Lord, and prayer for his return became an important and regular part of the service (cf. 1 Cor 11:26).

When Paul started out on his own preaching the gospel in the Hellenistic world, he included in it the bold assertion that Jesus Christ was Lord (cf. Rom 10:9). He did not borrow the title "Lord" from the non-Jewish savior-cults that abounded there, nor from the practice of emperor worship, in order to more easily ascribe divinity to Jesus. Rather, he proclaimed Jesus as Lord first of all because of the profound impact of Jesus upon his own life, and second, because he had already learned of this title for Jesus from his Palestinian fellow-Christians.

Thus from tradition and from personal experience Paul had come to understand that Jesus was indeed master not only of his individual life, but also of the church and of the world. He was eager, then, to let everyone know that Jesus is Lord supreme—the one Lord who stands above and over against however many lords the pagans may have named or believed in (1 Cor 8:5, 6).

Paul's meaning in "Jesus Christ is Lord"

The second question concerning what Paul had in mind when he used the title "Lord" to refer to Jesus—what did he mean?—is easier to answer. He meant at least by this title that Jesus was his master, and that he himself stood in relation to him as slave (*doulos*, Phil 1:1).

He understood, therefore, that he had only one course of action open to him—to obey the Lord Jesus Christ completely. This One had set the course of his life; Paul gladly and openly acknowledged that Jesus Christ was his Lord (3:8). He must act on Christ's commands. And if Paul recognized this relation for himself, he believed that it also applied equally to all others as well: "Before the name that Jesus bears," he wrote, "every knee will bow and every tongue confess that Jesus Christ is Lord" (2:10, 11). Especially is this true of Christians. They are those who presently acknowledge the Lordship of Jesus, and by such an acknowledgement they declare themselves his servants, people prepared to do his will (cf. Rom 10:9a; 14:8). With their ancient creed on their lips—"Jesus Christ is Lord"—they declare that their whole earthly existence belongs to him (cf. 1 Cor 6:13b), and that all relationships and actions take on new dimensions because of him (cf. Col 3:22-24). A person has no right then to call Jesus "Lord" and not do what he says (cf. Luke 6:46)—indeed that person cannot do so.

Yet paradoxically, from what Paul says elsewhere it is clear that to be a slave to this master was not the way to bondage. To be the Lord's slave is the only way to becoming a truly free person, one who is free from the tyranny of the law (Rom 7:1-6), of sin (Rom 6:18-22), of fear (Gal 4:8, 9) and of death (Rom 8:1-3).

One might say that Paul used "Lord" (kyrios) as a title for Jesus without intending thereby to equate Jesus with Yahweh (although in the Septuagint "Lord" [kyrios] was the Greek replacement for that sacred name), and without any intent to infringe on the idea of monotheism. Yet it is equally true that Paul wanted to convey to his friends at Philippi by the use of this term that Jesus was more than a mere human being. To be sure, in the letter to the Philippians Paul never addresses Jesus Christ directly either in prayer or thanksgiving. Nor does he direct his doxology to him. Only God the Father is the object of prayer and thanksgiving (1:3; 4:6), and only God the Father receives the doxology of praise (4:20).

In Philippians Paul is careful to distinguish between God the Father and the Lord Jesus Christ (1:2). He never calls Jesus "God" (theos), although he says Jesus existed "in the form of God" (2:6). He is careful to say that although the "fruit of righteousness" is produced by Jesus Christ, he adds that it is for the glory and praise of God (1:11). He calls Christians "children of God" (2:15), not "children of the Lord Jesus Christ." He notes that righteousness comes from God, but through faith in Jesus Christ (3:14). He says God is the source of peace, but the channel through which peace is conveyed to the Christian is Jesus Christ (4:7).

Paul acknowledges that Jesus Christ is to be confessed as Lord, but it is God who exalts him to this high position, and all this—the exaltation and confession—is *for* the glory of God the Father (2:9, 11).

This careful distinction on Paul's part between Jesus Christ and God the Father must be recognized. And yet Paul was convinced by revelation and personal experience that Jesus was more than simply a man; he was also divine.

But how could he say this? How could one who had lived his life so long under the influence of Jewish monotheism put this new insight and understanding into words? The use of the title "Lord" allowed him to give expression to this staggering idea. It is seen first in the salutation to the Philippians—"Grace and peace to you from God our Father *and* the Lord Jesus Christ" (1:2). Here Jesus Christ is clearly distinguished from God the Father. Yet since he is Lord he can nevertheless be designated as the co-source of grace and peace with God the Father. One is thus forced to say with Moule that:

> The position here occupied by Jesus in relation to God, as well as in many other opening formulae of the New Testament letters, is nothing short of astounding— especially when one considers that they are written by monotheistic Jews with reference to a figure of recently past history.[4]

With these words of salutation Paul has put the Lord Jesus Christ and God the Father on the same footing.

One should note too that when Paul concludes his letter to the Philippians, he bids them farewell by saying simply, "The grace of our Lord Jesus Christ be with you" (4:23). No longer is it "The grace of God the Father *and* the Lord Jesus Christ."

Observing this, one comes to realize that for Paul the Lord Jesus Christ has the right to perform the divine role of dispensing grace with full authority. He is here designated as the source of grace, the fountainhead of free saving love (*charis*). And he can bestow this grace freely on his church.

Further, Paul said that every creature in heaven, on earth, and under the earth will bow the knee before the Person who bears the name "Lord," and will openly acknowledge that it is Jesus who is this Lord (2:10, 11). Such an act of bowing the knee that Paul here calls attention to is *the* gesture of full inner submission in worship to the one before whom the knee is bowed (Kittel:Schlier).[5]

So when Paul says that this action will be done before Jesus as Lord, it is clear he meant to say, in this oblique way, that Jesus will be worshiped by every creature in the universe, that the Lord Jesus Christ is equally the object of worship with God. His intent becomes even more clear when one realizes that the latter part of the Christ-hymn (2:11) is in reality a quotation from the Old Testament where what originally was said of Yahweh is transferred now to Jesus:

> I am God, and there is no other. I have sworn by myself . . . that to me every knee will bow, every tongue will swear allegiance. (Isa 45:22b–23)

This staggering idea about Jesus Christ runs throughout Philippians helped on its way by the title "Lord." Paul, by using "Lord" of Jesus, has not the least desire to identify Jesus Christ with God the Father. He does not so much as hint at the possibility that Christ now usurps the place of God. He does not even breathe the words, "Jesus is God." And yet, because of his personal experience with Jesus Christ, although he cannot fully explain what is on his mind, he now knows nevertheless that Jesus Christ is certainly more than a mere human-being—and he wishes to tell his friends at Philippi of this.

So he proceeds to say, in effect, that if God is savior (Ps 106:21; Phil 1:28b), so is the Lord Jesus Christ (Phil 3:20).

The Person of Christ

If Yahweh-God is the source of joy (Neh 8:10), so is the Lord Jesus Christ (Phil 3:1; 4:4). If Yahweh-God is the stimulus to courage and strength (Josh 1:9), so is the Lord Jesus Christ (Phil 1:14; 2:30; 4:1). If Yahweh-God is near his people (Ps 119:151), so is the Lord Jesus (Phil 4:5). If God is to be loved and served with all one's mind, soul, and body (Deut 6:5; cf. Mark 12:30 par), and people are to press on to know Yahweh-God (Jer 31:34), so must it be with the Lord Jesus (Phil 3:8, 10). One feels the fervor of Paul for Christ as he pours out his soul to the Philippians telling them that he gladly counts everything he has received, owns, achieved, whatever—as loss, filth even, when compared to the sur-passingness of gaining Christ and of coming to know Christ Jesus as his Lord (3:7-10).

Summary

For Paul "Jesus"—this name by itself—was not an ade-quate name by which to give proper identification to the person who had blinded him with his majesty on the road to Damascus, and who, paradoxically at the same time, gave him sight to see and understand spiritual truths he had never dared dream of before.

"Christ" was a designation rich in meaning to Paul, and thus it was one he frequently used when talking to the Philippians about Jesus. "Christ"/"Messiah" was the fulfill-ment of the age-long expectation of the pious people of God. Their hopes and dreams of a thoroughly good king, of a ruler who would shatter the forces of evil and establish a righteous kingdom, a deliverer who would set the prisoner free, etc., had all been fulfilled now in Jesus.

Thus it is not surprising that Paul often combines these two names—"Jesus" and "Christ" into "Jesus Christ" or "Christ Jesus," the order seems to be of little consequence. By joining them in this way he enhances the meaning of both. Jesus is no longer merely a man from Nazareth, but he is the Christ, the looked-for Messiah. And the Messiah is no longer the expected one. Rather the Messiah has come and he is Jesus. Expectations have been fulfilled. Hopes have materialized. The dreams have become reality—Jesus is the Christ!

But not even this was adequate to express who Jesus is. Both "Jesus" and "Christ" are human names, which in themselves say little more than that this one was God's servant, one commissioned by God, one anointed with the Holy Spirit to do the will of God on earth. And if in some Old Testament passages—most frequently in those that have to do with the end-times—the Messiah-figure appears to be a supernatural being (cf. Dan 7:13, 14), yet this is still not meaning enough to explain adequately who Jesus is. The resurrection of Jesus Christ from among the dead told the earliest Christians that although he was indeed Messiah, the hope of Israel and of the world, he was more. And Paul's own encounter with this resurrected and living Jesus on the Damascus road convinced him, too, that Jesus was more than a man sent on a mission by God.

However it happened, "Lord" became the title that best described who Jesus was—the title which the earliest church settled upon (cf. Acts 2:32, 36), and which Paul delighted to use. It helped them to say that Jesus was divine, that he was God's vice-regent exercising the power that belongs to God, but even more, that he shared the very nature of God (recall that "Lord" in the Old Testament was *the* Greek word that translated Yahweh, and in the Hellenistic world was the title used to refer to deities of various kinds), without having to say in so many words that he was God. "Jesus Christ is Lord" became Paul's creed, perhaps the earliest creed of the church. As Lord he is to be served. As Master he is to be obeyed. Paul, therefore, set the whole course of his life to fulfill this obligation.

4 THE CHRIST-HYMN

The New Testament notes that from the earliest period of the church's history Christians were a singing people. They regularly instructed themselves by the use of psalms, hymns, and spiritual songs (Eph 5:19; Col 3:16). Originally their singing was of the Old Testament psalms. Soon, however, songs that were distinctively Christian began to be composed for use in worship and praise. Therefore, it is not surprising to learn that fragments or even whole sections of what seem to be very early Christian hymns have been found embedded in the writings of the New Testament (see Eph 5:14; Col 1:15–18; 1 Tim 3:16; 2 Tim 2:11–13; Rev 15:3, 4; 22:7). The most famous of these hymns is the beautiful hymn about Christ found at Philippians 2:6–11. It falls into two verses, one dealing with the humiliation of Christ (vv 6–8), and the other with the exaltation of Christ (vv 9–11).

Author of the hymn

Traditionally readers of this hymn have assumed that Paul wrote it as he wrote the other parts of Philippians. In recent times, however, this traditional assumption has been challenged, and arguments based on form, vocabulary, and christology have been set forth that point away from Paul as composer to someone other than the apostle. And yet, although Paul played down his own skill as speaker/writer (2 Cor 11:6), it is clear that he had the ability to clothe great ideas grandly (cf. 1 Cor 13), and that he had the rhetorical skill to write something as elegant as this hymn, if he chose to do so.

Furthermore, it is possible to point to passages that are unquestionably written by Paul where rare words or words used only once in the New Testament are found (cf. 1 Cor 4:10-13). So the fact that there are some words in this hymn found nowhere else in Paul's letters is hardly an argument against its being composed by him. And finally, the fact that the hymn does not say that Christ's death was a death "for us," nor refers at all to Christ's resurrection—themes that are central to Paul's christology—and the fact that Paul does not present Christ as the Servant of the Lord anywhere in his letters but here in the hymn, cannot in themselves prove that he did not write it. Does not context determine content? Could not the particular problems at Philippi addressed by this hymn have dictated its own special theme(s)?

There is thus no fully sufficient reason to depart from the traditional view that Paul composed this hymn. Its author, as Collange has written,

> must have possessed a genius which is not at everyone's disposal. As well as from the literary as from the theological point of view 2:6-11 concentrates into an exceeding concise poem considerable theological substance and is the work of a master.

It will be assumed from this point on that this master, the author of this hymn, was Paul.

Many different sources for the ideas expressed by this hymn have been suggested, only three of which can be mentioned here because of space. One suggested source is the gnostic Redeemed Redeemer myth. This myth describes the descent into this world of a "light-Person" from the highest god to bring knowledge (*gnōsis*) to the sons of light, who have sunk down into sleep and darkness. He comes to tell them who they are and to remind them of the light-world from which they fell. He teaches them, too, the secret passwords by which they can make their way safely back up through the demon-filled starry spheres to their heavenly home. He himself goes ahead and prepares the way for them, the way he also must take to be redeemed. For while he is on earth he does not appear in divine form, but rather in human form so as not to be recognized by the demons. Disguised in this way he must, like other humans, endure contempt and misery, pain and suffering until he leaves this world and ascends back to the world of light (Bultmann).[1] The difficulty with such a suggestion is that it is hard to date this gnostic myth, if not impossible. It might be very late. There is, thus, the very real possibility that the myth was itself created by the themes of the Christ-hymn rather than the other way around.

Another suggested source for the ideas of this Christ-hymn, and one that is quite popular today, is the Adam theme from the Old Testament.

Paul elsewhere makes good use of Adam, especially when he contrasts him with Christ, the Last Adam (cf. Rom 5:12–18; 1 Cor 15:21, 22, 45). It is suggested that Paul is doing the same here: Adam and Christ were both human beings made in the image of God (Gen 1:26; Phil 2:6—"image" and "form" are treated as synonymous). But whereas Adam grabbed at becoming like God, with the consequence that he lost his share in God's glory and became a slave, subject to corruption and death (Gen 3:5; 2:16, 17), Christ did not consider equality with God a prize to be snatched, and was therefore exalted by God (Phil 2:6).

Quite unlike Adam, who disobeyed (Gen 3:1–7), Christ chose the way of servanthood and mortality in obedience to God. The statement that Christ "emptied himself" (Phil 2:7) is thus interpreted to mean not that Christ gave anything away that he had, but rather that he freely chose to descend to the level of fallen humanity and, in obedience to God, to share the mortality and corruptibility of all such human beings (2:8). As a consequence, quite unlike the first Adam who was cast down out of paradise because of his self-seeking, the Last Adam, Christ, was lifted up and given the highest place because of his self-giving. God freely gave Christ that for which Adam grasped (Dunn, Ziesler.)[2]

The difficulty with suggesting such a source for the ideas of the hymn lies in the fact that those who suggest it must claim that there was a two-stage movement during the life of Jesus—(1) one stage in which he was Son, equal with God, in the sense that he was all that a person should be, a genuine human being, and (2) a second stage in which he consciously chose to become what he was not before, a person subject to death, now like other human beings in their humiliation.

Thus, in a sense he became less than a human being should be. But one is forced to ask when was this choice made? And how did Paul know about it? And why is it not mentioned elsewhere? And is this second stage properly described?

Is not the point being made much more striking and satisfying theologically if we understand Jesus on the cross not as less than fully human but as embodying and enacting that self-giving love which is the highest expression of human work and dignity—the point, in fact, where a human being most reflects the character of God himself? (Wright)[3]

Still another suggestion, one that is adopted here, is that the themes of the Christ-hymn were triggered by deep meditation by Paul on one particular event from the life of Christ as recorded in the Gospel tradition—Jesus' washing of his disciples' feet (John 13:3-17). This is not to say that Paul knew and used the fourth Gospel, but that he and the writer of that Gospel had access to the same information. The parallels in thought and in the progression of action between John 13:3-17 and Philippians 2:6-11 are striking. So precise, in fact, are these parallels that it is difficult to believe they are the result of mere coincidence.

Both the fourth evangelist and Paul writing in the Christ-hymn begin what they have to say in a similar fashion. John starts his narrative by saying that Jesus washed his disciples' feet because he knew that the Father had given everything into his hands and that he himself had come out from God and was going back to God (John 13:3), a remark that gives special emphasis to Jesus' act of humility. Paul, too, begins his hymn by saying that Jesus, being in the form of God and yet not taking advantage of his being equal with God, took the form of a slave, and did the work of a servant (Phil 2:6-8), a remark that equally emphasizes Jesus' act of humility. The entire hymn preserves the descent-ascent motif that is prominent in the Gospel story:

John 13:3-17	*Phil 2:6-11*
1. Jesus knows that he came out from God and was going back to God (v 3)	1. Jesus is in the form of God (v 6)
2. Jesus gets up from the table and lays aside his outer garments (v 4)	2. Jesus empties himself— lays aside his divine nature (v 7, Moffatt)

3. Jesus takes a towel and wraps it about himself, puts water in a basin and begins to wash his disciples' feet— the task of servants (1 Sam 25:41; cf. Mark 1:7) (v 5)	3. Jesus takes the form of a slave, and humbles himself (v 7)
4. Jesus finishes serving, takes again his outer garments, puts them on and sits down again at the head of the table from which he got up (v 12)	4. God exalts Jesus to the highest place and gives him the name above every name (v 9)
5. Jesus says: "You call me Lord and rightly so, for that is what I am" (v 13)	5. Every tongue is to call Jesus Christ, Lord (v 11)

It is also instructive to note that the purpose of John's account and of Paul's hymn is the same. The Johannine account is an acted parable to summarize the essence of Jesus' teaching: "Whoever wants to be great among you must be your servant, and whoever wants to hold the first place among you must be everybody's slave" (Mark 10:43, 44). The Philippian hymn powerfully illustrates Paul's teaching, which at this point is identical with that of Jesus' teaching: humble, self-sacrificing service to one another done in love is what is expected from a would-be follower of this Jesus (Phil 2:3, 4).

The purpose of the Christ-hymn

Paul's primary purpose for composing this hymn was not theological or christological but ethical. The goal he had in mind was not to give instruction in doctrine, but to reinforce instruction in Christian living. And he did this by using Christ as the ultimate model for moral action, as the supreme example of unselfish conduct. This is the most obvious and natural explanation for the appearance of the hymn at this particular point in the letter, that is, immediately after Paul's intense appeal to the Philippians to repent and to adopt a way of life quite in contrast to that which they were then in the course of pursuing (2:3, 4).

Nevertheless, in the process of reaching his primary objective—to alter patterns of living—Paul teaches profound truths both about the person of Christ and about the nature of God. He begins by declaring that before ever Christ became a human being, in his preexistent state, he was "in the form of God" (v 6). The phrase "in the form of God" is difficult to explain, if for no other reason than that the key word, "form" (morphē), occurs only two times in the New Testament and both times in this hymn (vv 6, 7). In spite of varying translations given for this word, ranging from "glory," "mode of being," "status," or "condition," to "image," with accompanying varying interpretations, it is possible to fall back on the basic meaning of the word, "form" (morphē), and proceed from there.

In very early Greek writings "form" (morphē) was used to express the way in which a thing, being what it is in itself, appears to one's senses. Morphē "always signifies a form which truly and fully expresses the being which underlies it" (MM). This word, "form" (morphē), then, would never be used of a wolf in sheep's clothing, for the outward appearance would not at all conform to what the creature really was in itself. So when this word is applied to God, his "form" (morphē) must refer to his deepest being, to what he is in himself, to that which cannot be reached by physical sight, because God is invisible. Cerfaux says of the word morphē: "In fact the word has meaning here only as referring to the reality of God's being."[4]

The Christ-Hymn

"The form of God," therefore, may be correctly understood as "the essential nature and character of God." This somewhat enigmatic expression appears, then, to be a cautious, oblique manner of speaking by which Paul says that Christ was God, possessing the very nature of God (cf. TEV, NIV, Goodspeed, Knox, Moffatt, Phillips) without his actually saying these precise words. It seems to be a statement made by one who perhaps, although reared as a strict monotheist and thus unable to bring himself to say, "Christ is God," was compelled, nonetheless, by the sheer force of personal encounter with the resurrected and living Christ to bear witness as best he could to the reality of Christ's divinity.

That this explanation is the correct one is confirmed by the expression, "to be equal with God," which immediately follows (v 6). Literally translated it is, "*the* being equal with God," where the definite article ("*the* being"), as it often does in Greek, points back to something previously mentioned. In this case the only thing it could point back to would be the words, "form of God." Therefore, the expression "being equal with God" is an equivalent way of saying "being in the form of God."

Still another difficulty in understanding the meaning of this hymn is the Greek word, *harpagmon*, in the sentence, "he did not consider that the being equal with God was *harpagmon*" (v 6). This word appears only this once in the New Testament, not at all in the Greek translation of the Old Testament, and very rarely in secular Greek. Hence, to understand precisely what it means here in the hymn is not an easy matter at all.

Some understand *harpagmon* to mean "a snatching after," "an act of aggression." To say then that Christ "thought it not robbery [*harpagmon*] to be equal with God" (KJV; see NIV, RSV) is to say that Christ, knowing himself to be equal with God, also knew that to be so was not the result of an act of aggression on his part. He knew equality with God was his by right, not by force.

Others have extended this basic idea of *harpagmon* — "aggressive action"—to give quite a different meaning to the hymn. These see "the being equal with God" as something not yet possessed but desirable nonetheless, a thing to be grasped after as Adam grasped after being like God (Gen 3:5). With such an interpretation the hymn is made to say that Christ was not equal with God, and what is more, he refused any temptation to use aggressive action to become so (cf. NEB).

Others understand *harpagmon* to mean "a thing to be clutched and held on to." Such an understanding of this word sees the hymn declaring that Christ already was equal with God by nature, and as such had no need to cling to this status as though it could be wrested from him (cf. JB).

Others yet argue that *harpagmon* is found here in the hymn in a standard Greek idiomatic expression that refers neither to an act of acquiring something by force, nor to an act of clinging to it greedily and selfishly. Rather this idiom refers to an *attitude*, a direction of mind that one has toward something that is already in one's possession. Thus in the hymn it is understood to mean that Christ's attitude was not such as to regard his equality with God as something to take advantage of, as something to be used for his own profit.

Still others explain the meaning of this difficult word and its implications for understanding the hymn as follows: *harpagmon* does not refer so much to a *thing* to be grasped, or to a *thing* to be clung to, as to the act of snatching itself—acquisitiveness, the desire to get and to have. Thus to consider oneself equal with God does not mean that one considers he has the right to take everything to himself, to grasp. When the hymn says that Christ "did not consider the being equal with God *harpagmon*," it intends to say that he did not at all believe his equality with God gave him the right to snatch, to grasp, to acquire everything for himself. Rather quite the contrary: "Jesus saw God-likeness essentially as giving and spending oneself out" (Moule).

In this connection, it is important to note that the participle at the beginning of verse 6—"who *being* in the form of God"—is often misleadingly translated as a concessive participle—"who *though he was* in the form of God" (RSV, NASB, Goodspeed, Williams). It should, however, on the basis of the context, more correctly be translated as a causative:

> Precisely *because [Christ] was* in the form of God he reckoned equality with God not as a matter of getting but of giving. (Moule)[5]

Perhaps the best explanation of the expression in which *harpagmon* is found is one which combines the last two suggestions made concerning it.

> In contrast with the standard picture of oriental despots, who understood their position as something to be used for their own advantage, Jesus understood his position to mean self-negation. . . . Divine equality does not mean "getting" but "giving": it is properly expressed in self-giving love. (Wright)[6]

Verses 6 and 7, then, can be paraphrased as follows: "Christ Jesus, who, because he was in the form of God, did not regard his equality with God as something to be used for his own advantage, but to be used for the advantage of others. Hence, he emptied himself. . . ."

This idea is clearly spelled out as the hymn progresses with a profound statement introduced by the conjunction "but"—"not that, *but* this." The being equal with God does not mean filling oneself up, but on the contrary it means emptying oneself out. Christ who shared the nature of God, who was equal with God, nevertheless emptied himself.

But what did this self-emptying entail? First, it is important to realize that the hymn never once says what Christ emptied himself of. One should thus keep from asking such questions. Second, it must be noted that "to empty" is but one of many meanings for the Greek verb (kenoō) which underlies this translation. It also means "to pour out." One can imagine, then, that Christ who was in very nature God, but who did not reckon that this nature was characterized by acquisitiveness "effaced all thought of self and poured out his fulness to enrich others" (Jones).[7] Here, in a poetic, hymn-like way Paul was saying what he had said more prosaically elsewhere—Christ put himself totally at the disposal of people; he became poor to make everybody rich (2 Cor 8:9; cf. Eph 1:23; 4:10).

This expression, "he emptied himself," is now defined more precisely by a series of participles—"*taking* the form of a slave," "*becoming* in the likeness of human beings," "*being* found in human form" (vv 7, 8). These participles express the way in which Christ emptied himself. Paradoxically this act of self-giving was accomplished by taking. Christ's self-emptying was achieved by becoming what he was not before, his kenōsis by adding to what he was, not by subtracting from it.

Jesus Christ voluntarily chose to pour himself out for others by taking the "form of a slave" (v 7). This does not mean that he merely disguised himself as a slave, having only the external markings of a slave. He really possessed the true character and attitude of a slave. That is to say, in the Incarnation the preexistent Christ entered the stream of human life as a person without advantage, claiming no rights or privileges of his own, for the express purpose of placing himself completely at the service of all people (cf. Mark 10:45).

Further, Christ poured himself out "by coming to be in

the likeness of human beings" (v 7). The one who always *was* in the form of God (v 6), now *becomes* a man—Paul uses here two very different verbs in two very different tenses to make this point clear. And the expression, "in the *likeness* of a man" with the one that immediately follows, "in human *form,*" are not used with any intent by the hymn writer to water down the genuineness of Christ's humanity, or to cast doubt on its reality. They are not meant to say that Christ only appeared to be a man or that he only took the outward form of a person as the gnostics later were to claim. Rather, these two expressions link up in hymnic fashion with that other expression, "*form* of a slave" (v 7). Together they become a threefold emphatic reiteration of one fundamentally important idea—that Christ in the Incarnation fully identified himself with humanity, that he became truly human both in appearance and in thought and feeling, that he shared people's plight genuinely. All these expressions together say in effect:

> Let there be no doubt—Christ was really and truly man, having to live the same kind of life as any other man had to live. (Grayston)[8]

Thus when the hymn mentions the self-emptying act of Christ, it does not put the emphasis upon what he gave up, but rather on what he added to himself—"the form of a servant," "the likeness of a man." It implies that at the Incarnation Christ became more than God, if this is conceivable, not less than God.

It is quite impossible to explain such a mystery—that the one who was in the form of God, equal with God, could also be a human person to the fullest, possessing all the potential for physical, mental, social, and spiritual growth that is proper to humanity, and be both at the same time—divine and human. And yet the Philippian hymn clearly sets forth just such a paradox and affirms it, but does not try to explain it.

The descent motif of the hymn, however, does not end here with the preexistent Christ becoming a truly human being. It goes on to say that as a man he humbled himself (v 8). Now this could mean merely that as a man Christ did not strive for some pinnacle of human achievement "where the battle was fought for honour, right and credit" (Barth).[9] It does mean that, but it means more than that, as the participle which follows makes abundantly clear: "He humbled himself *by becoming* obedient unto death" (v 8).

This concise phrase, "by becoming obedient unto death," describes the real nature of humility in general, and of Christ's humility in particular. True humility is to choose the will of God over one's own will. It is to decide to go God's way rather than one's own way. And in the case of Christ humility was for him to purpose radically to obey God, even at his own expense, even if it cost him his life to do so, even if he must die by crucifixion!

Now it is precisely at this point that there comes a striking change in the theme of the hymn—from descent to ascent, from humiliation to exaltation, from what Christ did, to what God did. The transition is marked by a strong inferential conjunction that means, "as a consequence, therefore," or "for this very reason." Christ, the one who was in the form of God, who was equal with God, emptied himself, putting himself in a position to serve human beings by becoming a human being, a servant, and humbled himself by setting himself strictly to obey God. This, then, is why God in one dramatic act exalted him, super-exalted him, and gave him the name "Lord" before which name every knee will bow.

This exaltation of Christ should not be thought of merely as a reward for his self-abnegation, or as a gracious gift bestowed by God on Christ which excludes any merit on his

The Christ-Hymn

part. Rather it is to be seen as the natural consequence of his humility. The inferential conjunction that begins this section, "as a consequence, therefore," points to an invariable law of God's kingdom: in the divine order of things, self-humbling leads inevitably to exaltation. It reflects the way things really are, the way the universe is made to work (cf. Matt 18:4; 23:12; Luke 14:11; 18:14).

But in this hymn the exaltation of Christ is more than the natural outcome of his self-giving, his self-humbling. It is above all the affirmation by God the Father that the Incarnation and death of Jesus were truly the ultimate revelation of divine love in action.

> In giving to Jesus the title [Lord], and in granting him to share that glory which, according to Isaiah xlv.23 (quoted in [Phil] 2:10), no one other than Israel's God is allowed to share, God the Father is as it were endorsing that interpretation of divine equality which, according to v 6, the Son adopted. (Wright)[10]

The hymn then is all of one piece. The person who ascended is the very one who descended. The exaltation of the crucified Jesus to the status of Lord at the end of the hymn is not to a position that only then became appropriate for him. It was his all along by virtue of who he was—from the very beginning he existed in the form of God, he was equal with God. Verse 11, the climax and end of the hymn, returns full circle to its start, tying the whole together by claiming the title Lord for him who from the first shared the very nature of God.

In this understanding of this exquisite hymn Jesus Christ is viewed as preexistent, divine, one equal with God, who nevertheless refused to take advantage of all this for his own personal gain. Instead, he is seen to empty himself, make himself powerless, pour himself out, put himself in a position by becoming human to serve people, set himself to obey God at any price. He is seen as considering his being equal with God "not as excusing him from the task of (redemptive) suffering and death, but actually as uniquely qualifying him for that vocation" (Wright).[11] That is why God exalted him and gave him the highest name in heaven and on earth—"Lord." Jesus Christ is Lord!

The hymn is not only about Christ, explaining in a remarkable way who he was, what he did, and his status now, but it is also a song about God. It makes crystal clear the true nature of God. Because God is Creator, Sovereign, Master, it is easy to assume that, since this is so, whatever God wants God gets. Hence, one might easily come to believe that the nature of God is to grasp, to reach out after everything and to hold it to himself. And one might also come to believe that God-likeness means having your own way, getting what you want (Moule).

The Christ of the hymn, however, shatters this misconception, showing that equality with God is precisely the opposite of this. Christ showed by his attitude and actions that for him to be in the form of God, to be equal with God, meant that he must give and spend himself out, that he must put himself at the disposal of others, that he must serve. Once again notice the force of the words of the hymn— "Who, precisely because he was in the form of God, did not consider that being equal with God meant taking everything to himself, but rather giving everything away for the sake of others" (2:6, 7). The hymn makes it unmistakably clear that contrary to whatever anyone may think about God, his *true* nature is characterized not by selfish grabbing, but by an open-handed giving.

Understood in this way the hymn fits perfectly in the context of chapter 2. Whereas the Philippians were acting selfishly, out of a spirit of rivalry, living in arrogance and pride, considering themselves better than others, taking care

The Christ-Hymn

of their own personal interests first, living with a grasping attitude (2:3, 4), Paul appeals to them as Christians, followers of the Christ, to show by their conduct that they are indeed Christian men and women, people belonging to Christ, indwelt by his Spirit, inspired by divine love (2:1). He asks them to think as Christ thought and to act as Christ acted, following the way of self-abnegation.

To understand that Christ's self-sacrificing attitude, his fundamental orientation toward sharing, giving, and serving—to know that all this is but the proper expression of divine character—is at the same time to understand the nature of Paul's appeal. It is not merely an appeal to imitate Christ. Rather, by its very nature it is an appeal reminding the Philippians that such a life of self-giving is in reality the outworking of the life of the Spirit of Christ within them.

> Though the word [*agapē* ("love")] is not used in the hymn itself, vv 6–8 might almost serve as a definition of what [love] means in practice—and vv 9–11 would then affirm that this love is none other than the love of God himself, at work supremely in Christ and now also, by his Spirit, in his people. The implication is clear: as God endorsed Jesus' interpretation of what equality with God meant in practice, so will he recognize self-giving love in his people as the true mark of life in the Spirit. (Wright)[12]

In other words, Paul calls upon the Philippians to follow Christ's example only because he knows that they through faith in Christ, share the nature of Christ, a nature God-like in character, marked by unselfishness.

5   THE CALL TO SALVATION

The words *salvation,* and *save,* mean different things to different people. Yet fundamental to all the various meanings is the basic idea of deliverance, freedom, release.

For example, Noah and all his family were "saved," meaning that they were delivered from death because of the impending flood (Heb 11:7). The Israelites were "saved," meaning that they were freed from slavery to the Pharaoh (Acts 7:25). The lame man at the Gate Beautiful was "saved," meaning that he was healed, freed from his crippling affliction (Acts 3:1-10; 4:12). Paul speaks of his own "salvation" when he refers to his expected release from prison (Phil 1:19). He challenges his Philippian friends to work out their "salvation," when he has primarily in mind that they take all necessary steps to restore to health and wholeness their church that had grown spiritually ill because of inner strife (2:12; 4:2, 3).

In the New Testament, however, the words "salvation," or

"save," are most frequently used in a religious sense. The reason for this is plain in the pages of the Bible: human beings fashioned in the likeness of God, formed to worship God and enjoy him, made to live in harmony with God and with one another, created to co-rule with God, to be crowned like God with glory and honor, find themselves instead estranged from God, hostile to God, dethroned, adrift in the world, alienated from God and from one another, slaves to fear, in bondage to death. They are people in need of salvation, i.e. of deliverance from that which has come between them and God, and of restoration to that ideal state from which they have departed (cf. Gen 3:23, 24; Isa 59:2).

The need for salvation

The culprit in all this, the cause of this "fall," is given a name—"sin." Sometimes in the New Testament sin is presented as though it were a separate entity, something quite apart from the individual, an evil power or force that controls one's actions against which the person stands quite helpless and from which he or she needs to be saved (cf. Rom 7:15-17).

More often, however, sin is defined as an individual's deliberate choice to turn away from God to that which is not God, to forget God, to exclude God, to replace God: "They exchanged the truth about God for a lie and worshipped and served the creature rather than the Creator" (Rom 1:25). Sin is a choice against God resulting in idolatry. It is a choice for which people are culpable and for which they will pay the tragic price—a darkening mind, an inability to distinguish good from evil, a lack of any capacity to halt a steady decline toward wickedness and perversion, and the powerlessness to avert death at the end. Sin is a break in relations between God and people, which results in a loss of human freedom, and an involvement in human bondage (see Rom 1:21–31; 6:19, 20, 23).

Now this is not an isolated problem, or the problem of only a few. It is a universal problem: "All have sinned and come short of the glory of God" (Rom 3:23). All suffer from a fatal flaw, a failure of moral nerve. All thus are helpless to help themselves (cf. Rom 5:6). All stand under the judgment of God, under the wrath of God (Rom 1:18; 5:9). All are destined to reap the harvest of sin since all are appointed to die (Rom 6:23). This then is the fundamental human predicament from which everyone needs to be saved, delivered, released.

Against this dark backdrop Paul's remarks in the Philippian letter about salvation are to be understood, especially as they are expressed in chapter 3. True, Paul does not here use the words "save," "salvation," "savior," but the idea of salvation is paramount in his thinking as he draws back the curtain on his personal life. Here he shares with his friends in a most intimate way the beguiling nature of sin and its devastating consequences, and then declares how it can be conquered and the sinner set free.

Put simply, Paul is saying here, in effect: "Look! People are sinful with all that that entails [see above]. They cannot, therefore, extricate themselves or save themselves from this ultimate predicament by their own moral effort. What is humanly impossible is divinely possible. God himself acts to save. God does it by himself in his own way and tolerates no competition. God does it by Christ and by faith in Christ."

If Paul begins this section with harsh words against the Jews (3:2), it is not because he hates them and wishes to put them down. Rather it is because he loves them and wishes them to be saved (cf. Rom 9:1–4). The Jews of Paul's day were a people intent on keeping God's law. Their sense of well-being, therefore, in the apostle's mind, was due in large part to the fact that they believed they were performing accurately the works demanded by that law. They thus perceived themselves to be good people, doers of what is good and right. Astonishingly Paul calls them instead, "evil workers" (3:2). Why? He does it not because he believed that what they were doing was morally wrong. Rather, he does it because he had come to realize that their reliance on "works" was in the end fatal for them—fatal in that such reliance is ultimately self-reliance, idolatry, an attitude toward life that tends to obscure or eliminate the need for God who alone is the source of true life and goodness.

If Paul continues this section by denouncing "confidence in human achievement" (3:3) he does so not to speak ill of human accomplishments or to advocate that people make no attempt to achieve. He does it rather to reaffirm what he said earlier when he called the Jews "workers of evil" (3:2). The very human tendency to believe that one can achieve a proper standing with God and earn God's favor by doing something, however great or good, is folly.

The word Paul uses here for "human achievement" is the Greek word, *sarx*, literally "flesh." It pictures a person at his or her highest and best, striving to achieve an adequate status before God, but without dependence upon God. It pictures people as relying on their own ability to do the will of God and to attain the goodness that God requires without realizing that such goodness can be attained only by abandoning self and throwing oneself wholly on the mercy and grace of God. *Sarx* is that self-reliance, that confidence in one's own capacity to please God and earn a favorable verdict from the Judge which causes Paul to strike out so hard against it. Such confidence in human achievement (*sarx*) is futile.

If Paul fills out this section now with a lengthy recitation of his own status and accomplishments, it is not to call attention to what a good fellow he is. It is rather to underscore again his fundamental thesis and to give concrete proof of its correctness: No one can rely on human privilege and position or personal achievement to gain favor with God. If anyone could do this, surely he, Paul, could. He had the right pedigree, and had done all the right things (3:4–6).

But Paul, through a dramatic personal experience, which he does not explain here (see the Introduction), had been forced to make a profound reevaluation of his own values. He came to see with horror that the things he had previously viewed as benefiting him had in reality been working to destroy him by blinding him to his need for the true righteousness that God requires and that God alone could supply. He understands now that all his struggle as a religious person to be good enough was a pure and simple usurpation of God's prerogatives. Hence, with abhorrence he counts everything he once valued as loss, filth even, and turns from it forever.

God's way of salvation

What then is one to do? How can one nullify the effects of sin? How is one to extricate himself from the mortal predicament in which he finds himself? How can one become good enough for God? What can one do to earn God's favor? How can people save themselves? Paul's answer to these questions is simply, "Nothing!" But lest one despair at such an answer, he hastens to add that though the sinner can do nothing to repair the breach, God has done everything necessary. Prompted by his great love God has acted to save sinners (Rom. 5:8).

Paul does not use the word *salvation* (*sōtēria*) here in Philippians chapter 3, perhaps because for him the terms "savior," "to save," and "salvation" belong properly to the end-times, to the consummation of the age. Instead, when he refers to Christians' present status he prefers to use a word that includes but exceeds the ideas contained in *salvation*. He uses the word "righteousness" (*dikaiosynē*), a favorite of his which he borrowed from the Old Testament (cf. Isa 45:21; 46:13; 51:5, *passim*) and then enlarged upon. He uses it to describe not only the release of sinners from the bondage to their sin, but in effect, to refer to the total undoing of sin.

"Righteousness" for Paul is the giving back to people that which sin took from them, the ultimate goodness which God demands, the raising of human beings to that standard of their humanity originally divinely designed for them, the full restoration of people to their right and proper relationship with God, reconciliation!

This kind of righteousness, however, Paul now knows is a righteousness that cannot be achieved by human endeavor. It is the "righteousness of God" (Phil 3:9; cf. Rom 1:17). That is to say, it is the righteousness that originates with God. God has taken the initiative to provide this righteousness because of his great love for people. It is his free gift to people which they cannot buy, which they cannot earn, which they cannot merit. Thus after years of ignorant struggle on his own part Paul is finally able to say with relief that he no longer has any intention or desire to be found (at the day of judgment?) having only his own righteousness, his own goodness to present to God, a goodness earned by diligently keeping the law (3:9). Rather, he now possesses and wants to be found (at the day of judgment?) having the true righteousness that God himself supplies—the only righteousness that will stand the final test.

God has acted to save, to accept back his erring, wandering, alienated people and to restore them to fellowship with himself. But how did he do this? Paul says he did it through Christ (3:9)—the person of Christ is positively essential in making this righteousness available to all. And although Paul does not explain here how this is so, he does this elsewhere (Rom, Gal), and it is contained in the gospel. The gospel he preached he called the gospel of God (Rom 15:16; 1 Thess

2:2), or the gospel of Christ (Rom 15:19; Phil 1:27), by which he meant good news about God's action to save the world of mankind through the person and work of Jesus Christ. Hence, the Philippians, who had heard the gospel, understood exactly what he meant when he wrote to them so concisely of God's righteousness given through faith in Christ (3:9)—Christ, though existing in the form of God, equal with God, nevertheless emptied himself and became a human being. In this way he placed himself in a position by which as the Anointed of the Lord he could come to grips with human sin and dethrone it. He could thus encounter the demands of God's law and fulfill them, face the wrath of God against sin and avert it from the sinner, challenge the celestial or infernal powers and overthrow them, submit to death and destroy it, and hear the will of God and do it (cf. Rom 5:6-9; 10:4; Col 2:13-15; Phil 2:8; cf. Heb 2:14, 15).

The person of Christ is crucially central to the gospel. By him—the incarnate God—and by him only, by virtue of his unique nature, his perfect life, his obedient death, and his triumphant resurrection, God has worked to reconcile people to himself, to redeem them from the bondage of sin, to lead them out of darkness into light, out of death into life. All that people could not do for themselves, because they were weak, helpless, ungodly, and enemies, God has done for them at immense cost to himself (see Phil 2:6-11; Rom 1:17; 3:21-28; 5:6; 6:20-23; 8:37-39; 2 Cor 5:18-20; Gal 3:13; 4:3-7; Col 1:12-22).

In a truly amazing way, never fully explained by Paul, the Christ-event—the life and death of Christ (i.e. his self-sacrifice for human sin), and his resurrection—released into this fallen world the supreme power by which God can act in love to make his enemies his friends, by which he can act to reconcile sinners to himself (cf. 2 Cor 5:18, 19). This is not only the word of Paul, but the consistent testimony of the church from the time of Jesus' first disciples until today.

God, then, has provided for all people the required righteousness, which is his righteousness. And he has done this through Christ alone. But his wish is not that people have this righteousness thrust upon them, but that they choose to accept his gift with gladness and gratitude. This act of acceptance of God's offer Paul calls faith. Hence, he continues his remarks here with the words, "the righteousness of God is made available *through faith in Christ*" (Phil 3:9).

Paul saw faith (*pistis*) not as an alternative way for human beings to achieve God's favor by their own efforts, a new kind of deserving work, but as quite the opposite of this. Faith is, in effect, an admission that one cannot earn God's approval by what he does, but can only take God's free offer of forgiveness and grace and love. And since God's offer is made by virtue of the life and above all by virtue of the death and resurrection of Christ, the righteousness, the condition of being truly right with God, must come *through faith in Christ*.

Faith in Christ, therefore, in the strictest sense is not intellectual assent to a series of propositions about Christ, or beliefs about Christ. It is the act of personal trust and self-surrender to Christ. It is the movement of one's whole soul in confidence out toward Christ. It is the reaching out and accepting of Christ's having done for people what they could never do for themselves. It is the "Yes!" of one's whole personality to the personal address of Christ. It embraces both an initial positive response to Christ, and a continuing attitude of trust in and commitment to him.

When Paul came to understand this, that in Christ God had already anticipated him, that in Christ God had already looked with favor on him (long before ever he had lifted a finger to gain this favor), that in Christ God had already been gracious and merciful toward him, that in Christ God had already acted to reconcile him to himself, and that in Christ God had already accepted him unreservedly—when he understood all this he could make no other response than the response of faith, accepting this offered gift in humility and thankfulness. With a sense of deep gratitude he once and for all became Christ's devoted follower. Thus it is that he wrote with such intensity:

> I count everything as loss because of the one supreme value, namely to know Christ Jesus my Lord. For him I did in fact lose everything. But I consider it all as unspeakable filth for the goal of gaining Christ. Yes, I consider everything as unspeakable filth for the goal of knowing Christ in the power of his resurrection and in the fellowship of his sufferings. (3:8–10)

Paul's most fundamental need, and that of every human being—to be reconciled to God—had been fully and completely met in Christ. Hence, he knew that he could afford to surrender everything else, but *not* Christ. From the moment he understood this, he never wavered in his fidelity to the decision he made regarding Christ.

Philippians chapter 3 is Paul's most thoroughly personal explanation of salvation in this letter. And it is presented here not as a salvation that is solely future in its dimensions, but very much a present thing. The salvation or righteousness of God under discussion is salvation/righteousness immediately available. That is to say, people do not need to wait until the end of time to find out if they have been accepted by God. God accepts people today, now, just as they are, because of the fact of Christ.

But salvation in the ultimate sense is eschatological. It does not belong only to the "now" period. Thus Paul more than once makes reference to the Day of Christ or the Day of Christ Jesus in his letter to the Philippians (1:6, 10; 2:16).

The Call to Salvation

By this expression he means the end of the world, the consummation of time, the goal of history, which the Old Testament writers designated as the Day of the Lord. The Old Testament writers often viewed it as a day of wrath and judgment (Isa 2:10–22; Joel 3:12–16a), a day to be dreaded, because God, who is righteous, stands threateningly opposed to all human unrighteousness and ungodliness (see Rom 1:18; 3:9–18; cf. Eph 2:3) of both Gentile and Jew alike (Rom 1:18–32; 2:8–9).

But Paul views it no longer with terror or distress. Why? Because as he says elsewhere, Christ has taken the full brunt of the divine wrath and the divine judgment against sin upon himself, thereby making it possible for God to remain righteous even while he acquits the unrighteous (Rom 3:24–26).

The cross of Christ, therefore, becomes for Paul both the supreme revelation of the "wrath of God" against sin (Rom 1:18; 2 Cor 5:21), and of the inexhaustible love, mercy, grace, and forgiveness of God by which he reconciles sinners to himself rather than drives them away from him to destruction (cf. Eph 2:16). Hence, the Day of Christ is for Paul and for Christians not a day to be dreaded, but to be anticipated with fullness of joy, because it is a day when they can expect the arrival of one who is both friend and savior.

Paul writes of this anticipation in 3:20: "For our citizenship is in heaven, and from heaven we eagerly wait for a savior, the Lord Jesus Christ" (cf. also 3:11 where he refers passingly to the resurrection).

This final appearance of Christ will herald the completion of God's saving work on earth. What began with the provision of a proper standing before God effected through the first coming of Christ, by his life, death, and resurrection, is now to be capped off with the transformation of the total person (*sōma*) at Christ's second coming—"the Lord Jesus will transform our bodies of humiliation so that they may become like his glorious body," i.e. spiritual bodies, bodies inherently alive, no longer subject to corruption and dying (3:21; cf. 1 Cor 15:42-50).

Every trace of the person's moral weakness, physical feebleness, and mortality will be removed. Salvation in the ultimate sense, then, is not negative only—deliverance from sin and death—but positive too. It includes the exchange of weakness for strength, death for life, humility for glory. And the Savior, the Lord Jesus Christ, will bring about this radical transformation by the exertion of that same power which he uses to subdue all things, the entire universe, to himself (3:21; cf. Col 1:29). There is thus no need to be anxious that the power to save will ever be inadequate.

Salvation or destruction

Salvation also implies nonsalvation. If God has acted in mercy and grace to save sinners by Christ's death and resurrection, and if he has dignified people with the freedom to choose life or its opposite, i.e. to exercise faith or to refuse to believe, then it is not surprising to learn that Paul warns the Philippians of those who have chosen against God— "They are enemies of the cross of Christ, their god is their appetite, they esteem only what is shameful, their concern is for earthly things, they are people horizon-bound in their thinking" (3:18-19).

Without trying at this point to identify these people, except to say that they may possibly be religious people concerned with certain rituals that affect the body, and without commenting at all on their moral behavior, it is nevertheless correct to point out that for the apostle they are people who reject the good news of God's having acted to save them through Christ. They are people who are concerned with values that pass away, with values that have neither divine origin or lasting qualities.

Hence, instead of salvation their end is perdition, loss,

destruction—which is banishment from God who is life (3:19). What stands as a judgment against them becomes a warning to everyone. There exists the tragic possibility of exchanging the glorious immortal God for some lesser deity. Strangely, this potential has the greatest chance of becoming reality in the realm of the religious, where doctrine and ritual so easily become that to which people wholly devote themselves and to which they commit themselves completely. In this way they become idolaters (cf. Rom 1:21–23).

6   THE CHRISTIAN LIFE

Sanctification

As has been noted, Paul rarely uses the terms *to save* and *salvation*, except in contexts where he is referring "to the final stage of the work begun by God through Jesus Christ, namely [the] decisive laying aside of the coming wrath (Rom 5:9; 1 Cor 3:15; 5:5; 1 Thess 5:9)" (Collange).[1] And it is often pointed out, too, that the words that Paul regularly uses to describe the present status of Christians—"to justify," "justification"—do not refer to a positive and qualitative change in the person justified. "Justification is strictly acceptance [by God], restoration to fellowship [with God], and not transformation of character" (Ziesler).[2]

Remarks like these may lead one to conclude that salvation/justification has only to do with deliverance from the consequences of sin, that is, from the wrath of God, from eternal death, not at all with the present inner alteration of one's person and an accompanying alteration in thinking and conduct.

Nothing, however, could be farther from Paul's mind than such a conclusion. In the words of George MacDonald,

> The notion that the salvation of Jesus is [only] a salvation from the consequences of our sins, is a false, mean, low notion. The salvation of Christ is salvation from the smallest tendency or leaning to sin. It is a deliverance into the pure air of God's ways of thinking and feeling. It is a salvation that makes the heart pure, with the will and choice of the heart to be pure. To such a heart, sin is disgusting. It sees a thing as it is— that is, as God sees it, for God sees everything as it is. . . . Jesus did not die [merely] to save us from punishment; he was called Jesus because he should save his people from their sins.

And if Paul's words "salvation" and "justification" should in themselves happen to be technical terms with rather narrow meanings, yet it is clear from the whole of Paul's message that restoration to a right relationship with God (justification) is a meaningless term unless it is accompanied by a transformation of character. It is the goal of God's action in Christ to recreate people in his image and likeness, to make the sinner a saint, the evil person good, the base, upright and noble (cf. 2 Cor 5:17; Col 3:10). In the language of theology this continuing divine process toward goodness in this present life is called sanctification.

The context of sanctification

Paul's letter to the Philippians is an ideal letter to study in order to gain an understanding of the meaning of sanctification. The Philippians had been brought into proper relationship with God in Christ. They partook of Christ's righteousness by virtue of their incorporation into him. It was not that God treated them "as if" they were righteous. In Christ they were indeed righteous.

But this righteousness has to be understood in light of the entire New Testament conception of eschatology. This is to say, that while the righteousness of God is something that properly belongs to the end of time, yet it can be grasped by faith and revealed by faith even now in the present time. The Philippians lived "between the times," so to speak, between the first and final comings of Christ and they partook of the character of two eras—this present age and the age to come. By faith, eschatologically, they were righteous—as righteous as ever they would be when the world ends and the new day dawns, because in Christ they were already in the new age. But as people living in the present age they were still experiencing the powers of darkness and evil pressing in upon them. Righteousness was both something that the Philippians already had, and also something for which they still waited (cf. Gal 5:5). They possessed it but not as they would hereafter.

> The "saint" of NT theology is not a perfected being but a forgiven sinner, and sanctification (. . . the state of holiness), like [righteousness], is an eschatological reality, not a simple possibility for Christians who are still subject to the "powers" of this age, even though in principle those powers are defeated. Christians are indeed [saints] . . . ; nevertheless it is only by prayer and striving and by the power of the Spirit that the eschatological [holiness] (2 Cor. 1.12; Heb. 12.10) and [righteousness] . . . can be manifested even to the eyes of faith in this mortal life (2 Cor. 4.7-18). (Richardson)[3]

Divine/human elements in sanctification

Nowhere is this paradoxical nature of the Christian life more clearly illustrated than in Paul's letter to the Philippians.

The Christian Life

Nowhere are the two ideas of justification (what Christians *are* by virtue of their being in Christ), and sanctification (what Christians *are becoming* by virtue of their own striving and by the enabling power of the Spirit) articulated more forcefully than here.

To begin this study it is worth noting that Paul right off affirms the fact that Christians are "saints," "holy people" (*hagioi*, 1:1). They are this because they are in Christ (1:1) and not because of their own efforts to be good. And yet paradoxically, by using this very term Paul makes it clear that Christians are not exempt from any kind of moral endeavor. "Saints" (*hagioi*) is a technical term by which Paul informs Christians that they are "God's special people," and as such are responsible to become like God. If God is himself holy, i.e., perfect in purity and goodness and justice and love (cf. Lev 19:2–18), then as "holy ones," that is, as God's own people, Christians must strive to be like God in character and conduct (cf. 1 Pet 1:16).

In other words, relationship to God demands a proper ethical response. Thus, at the very beginning of this letter Christians are not only informed of who they *are* because of what God has done for them in Christ, but of what they *are to become* by means of their own moral struggles. The highest calling for Christians is stated immediately, and the course is set for the direction along which the activity of their entire lives must proceed.

Further, the implication of Paul's prayer in 1:9–11—"I pray that your love may keep on increasing still more and more . . . in order that you may be filled with the fruit of righteousness that Jesus Christ produces"—is that Christians are people characterized by love (*agapē*), and goodness (*dikaiosynē*). This is to say, they are people who are ready to sacrifice and serve, to give and forgive, to help and sympathize, to lift up the fallen and restore the broken (cf. Rom

12:9, 10; 1 Cor 13:4-7; Gal 5:25). And they are such because they have been transformed by the power of God and are kept productive in love and goodness by the generative power of Christ (Phil 1:11).

And yet the very writing down of this prayer and the sending of it along in the letter indicate that it was not only an *appeal* to God to act for the Philippians, but an *exhortation* to the Philippians to act in their own behalf. Certainly the apostle intended the Philippians to overhear, as it were, what he had to say to God about them.

Once again, then, the dual nature of the Christian life becomes evident—God works and the Christian must work. God initiates love and fosters it, but the Christian is coresponsible with God for its increase. Together they work to take love beyond mere feeling and desire, beyond intention solely, into a dynamic, ever-increasing action that discriminatingly seeks out the best for everyone and harm to no one (Phil 1:9-11; cf. Rom 13:8-10; Gal 5:13).

The clearest, most unambiguous statement of God's intent to incorporate human volition and action into his divine plan to achieve personal and corporate goodness is made by Paul in Phil 2:12, 13: "Work out your own salvation with fear and trembling; for it is God who is at work in you both to will and to do his good pleasure."

The word "salvation" that Paul uses here is not to be understood in a theological sense referring to the eternal salvation of the human soul, but in the less ultimate sense of the restoration of an ailing church to health. And here it is not the individual believer who is being called upon "to a personal application of salvation" (Müller).[4] Rather, the entire Christian community (note that the "you" is plural here) is being charged with responsibly taking whatever steps are needed to recover wholeness. The context favors this latter understanding of the word "salvation," for 1:27-2:4 details symptoms of a serious malady that had seized the Christian community at Philippi, a spiritual illness from which it needed to be delivered.

Because the Philippians, as all Christians, were living between two ages—this present evil age and the new age of righteousness—and were partaking of the character of both, they were still capable of being motivated by party spirit, selfishness, conceit, pride and arrogance. All of these are negative qualities that destroy unity and tear people apart from one another (2:2–4).

On the other hand, the Philippians had been recreated by the power of God. They thus had been freed from the powers of the kingdom of darkness, this age, and delivered into the kingdom of light and love—the new age (cf. Col 1:12, 13). As a consequence it was possible for Paul to appeal to them to get busy and work out their own salvation. In effect, he was saying:

> You chose to yield to the forces of evil that have wreaked havoc in your church. Now you can also choose to resist these forces, to withstand them, to go on the offensive against them for good. And furthermore, as those belonging to the new age of righteousness you must!
>
> Therefore, obey and begin to work at achieving spiritual health among yourselves (2:12). Stop grumbling. Stop arguing (2:14). Hurry! You do not have to wait for my coming. Get busy, for it is God, not I, who presides over this renewal and it is he who is effectively at work among you creating both the desire and the drive to promote good will toward one another. (2:12, 13)

Hence, it is clear that Christians individually and corporately have a very large part to play in the steady maintenance and strengthening of the new life which they have received from God as the result of Christ's death and resurrection.

They too are very much responsible for that continuous, constant, plodding progress toward goodness of character translated into goodness of conduct called "sanctification." Christians are given no encouragement whatever to say, "This work of sanctification is God's responsibility, not ours; it is the work of the Holy Spirit, not ours." Christians are to act. True, they are to act with humility and respect, with fear and trembling (2:12), but they are to act nonetheless. Christians are responsible for whether or not they make progress in righteousness, whether or not they become increasingly good people.

While agreeing that this is true, one must nevertheless recognize and allow for this fact that Collange points out:

> [In 2:13 Paul] gives God [the] dominant place at the very heart of human activity; he it is who "energizes" the action of man and even motivates it. But it must be noticed that Paul does not state this truth in a *restrictive* sense as though putting a bridle upon human freedom, but rather with a *positive, outgoing* meaning; henceforward no obstacle can any longer shackle the efforts of men "directed at mutual good will" since God himself is at work in these efforts. Divine action does not curtail human action but rather provokes a reaction which it supports.

Finally, then, and by way of summary, because Paul understands the ambiguous position in which Christians find themselves—between two ages, this age and the age to come—he understands the nature of Christians: They are people who partake of the characteristics of both worlds.

Hence he is able to acknowledge the fact, and not be surprised or shocked by it, that Christians are indeed capable of allowing themselves to be motivated by jealousy and quarrelsomeness (1:15). He knows that Christians can and do intentionally hurt one another because of personal ambition (1:17). He is quite aware that Christians can and do act selfishly, arrogantly, looking out for their own interests, not those of others or of Jesus Christ (2:3, 21). He realizes that Christians can and do fight among themselves and create disharmony and disunity within the community of faith (4:2). He understands that Christians can and do grumble and complain (2:14), and worry and are anxious (4:6). He is indeed ready to recognize the hard facts of life in this world—the unpleasant things about Christians that everyone would like to forget. Paul refuses to hide such weaknesses as though they did not exist.

Nevertheless he is unwilling to accept or be tolerant with the status quo. Christians are also responsible for change and growth within themselves. Hence, the abundance of imperatives in Philippians:

- conduct yourselves in a manner worthy of the gospel of Christ (1:27)
- strive for unity (2:2)
- do nothing from selfishness (2:3)
- look out for the interests of others (2:3)
- live in harmony (4:1, 2)
- help those in need (4:3)
- stop being anxious (4:6), and so on.

Christ died not only to save people from the consequences of their sin, but from their sins. God's action to save people through Christ was designed ultimately to make them good, and doers of that which is good. God's intent in the cross was to create a community of caring people, a group of people characterized by love, people who could never be blamed for having harmed anyone, only applauded for shining as lights in the darkness, for being children of God, i.e., people of goodness, in a world of corrupt and sinful men and women (2:15).

Since sanctification is so very important and includes human effort, Paul is concerned that this effort not be left to chance or intuition. He wants the Philippians to know what they can do, what steps they can take to guarantee their progress in the Christian faith and life. The advice he gives the Philippians is of such a nature that it can be made good use of by Christians in all generations.

For one thing, he tells them to forget the past (3:13). Recollection of wrongs done in the past, of past failures and sins can impede Christian growth. If these are allowed to fill one's mind they have the capacity to paralyze with guilt or to fill one with despair. It is possible to forget past sins and faults, because God, in effect, has said in Christ: "I love you; I forgive you; I heal you. Sin is one very important reason you need me. I have acted to remove it from you. So forget this part of your past!"

Furthermore, recollecting past attainments, permitting the mind to dwell upon successes and achievements can also retard Christian development. It may give Christians the false belief that they can put life in neutral and say, "We have arrived" (cf. 3:12). So forget the past, Paul urges. Forget it in such a way that the past, good or bad, will have no negative bearing on one's present spiritual growth.

Second, Paul encourages the Philippians (Christians) to live full out, to live straining toward what is ahead, to race for the finish line! (3:13, 14). The words Paul chose in order to give this piece of advice come from the athletic contests. One of them is a rare word, used only here in the New Testament. Literally it means "to stretch full out" (*epekteinomai*). It pictures the Christian as a runner in the Olympic games with his body bent over, his hand outstretched, his head fixed forward, his eyes fastened on the goal (Vincent).

　　　　　　　　　　　　　　The Christian Life

This word powerfully describes the need for concentration, for prodigious effort, and for the determination not to quit. Vividly it portrays the ceaseless personal exertion and the intensity of desire that a person must have if he wishes to reach the goal—the high calling of God.

The other word, too, (diōkō, "I press on," "I run") underscores what has already been communicated by the verb "to stretch full out," reinforcing the idea that the Christian life can never be thought of as static, but dynamic. This word also focuses on the necessity for striving, for constantly pursuing, for resolute determination in order to make life's aim—Christ-like character and conduct—a reality. Thus, to be a true Christian is no easy matter; it is a difficult, challenging life that calls forth people's greatest courage and moral strength. In some respects it would be easier to give one's life blood once for all than drop by drop in the daily struggle of life. Most Christians, however, are called upon to travel this more difficult way.

These two pieces of advice in one sense were Paul's motto for living. They together became the focus of his life:

I concentrate on this; I forget all that lies behind me and with hands outstretched to whatever lies ahead I go straight for the goal—my reward the honor of my high calling by God in Christ Jesus. (3:13, 14 Phillips)

Third, Paul says, "Pray!" (4:6).

How do people gain and keep their equilibrium in a world heaving with anxiety-creating situations? How do Christians keep their balance? How do they ward off worries that sap their growth in the faith? Paul's answer? By prayer! Believing that God is, that he is greater than the greatest problem, that he is deeply interested in Christian development, and that he is the rewarder of those who earnestly seek him (cf. Heb 11:6), Paul emphatically urges the Philippians to find release from their anxieties in prayer and more prayer.

From personal experience Paul had learned that "the way to be anxious about nothing was to be prayerful about everything" (Jones).[5] So he writes to the Philippians, "Let God know what is troubling you" (4:6). This may seem a rather quaint way Paul has of broaching the subject of prayer, "Let God know"—as though God needed to be informed about anything. Paul is telling the Philippians that while they must never think of prayer as a means of manipulating God, or as a way of pressuring God to do what they want—as a magic lamp, so to speak, rubbed to put God at their service—prayer is nevertheless to be cherished. Prayer is an opportunity to give expression to their concerns, to put into words their desires, to articulate their deepest yearnings.

Paul is saying, in effect, that prayer is a conversation with a person, in this case the supreme Person of the universe—"*Let your request be made known to God.*" Why? Because God hears, knows, understands, cares about, and will respond as he knows best to those things that could otherwise sink people in despair and stunt their growth as Christians.

But when Christians bring their petitions to God, they may discover that many of these anxious prayers wither away under his judgment, seen there for what they are—simply selfish requests. And if this happens, these, then, may be replaced with true prayers, prayers for grace to accept what is, or for the courage and strength to team up with God to change what must be changed.

"And pray with thanksgiving," Paul continues (4:6). "Be grateful." Gratitude to God is a very big thing to Paul as can be seen from Romans 1:21, and from reading Paul's own prayers (cf. Phil 1:3, 4).

To begin by praising God for the fact that in *this* situation, as it is, he is so mightily God—such a beginning is the end of anxiety. To be anxious means that we ourselves suffer, ourselves groan, ourselves seek to see ahead. Thanksgiving means giving God the glory in everything, making room for him, casting our care on him, letting it be his care. The troubles that exercise us then cease to be hidden and bottled up. They are, so to speak, laid open to God, spread out before him. (Barth)[6]

As a result of bringing one's anxieties to God in prayer, Paul then writes, "the peace of God will guard your innermost selves" (4:7). God's peace (*eirēnē*) about which Paul is here referring is not mere calmness and serenity. Rather, it is that which reaches out and creates health, harmony, and wholeness. This peace is the fundamental mark of the messianic kingdom (cf. Isa 9:6, 7), nearly synonymous with messianic salvation (Acts 10:36; Eph 2:17; 6:15; cf. Isa 52:7).

Peace, then, is characteristic of the new age to come, the age of the Messiah (Christ), the age to which Christians now belong. It is that wholeness of the self, that health of the soul, that harmony within a person and with God that should characterize Christians to such an extent that their personal goodness will work creatively to benefit that part of the world in which they find themselves. So pray! And what begins with people informing God about their anxieties ends with God letting them know what really matters to him and filling their minds with peace, his creative, health-bringing calmness of soul that frees them to think rightly and to take hold cooperatively with him to help answer their own prayers.

Fourth, in a section where Paul focuses on moral excellence (*aretē*—the highest good of human beings) as a worthy goal for which Christians should strive, he adds two further steps toward achieving. They fairly well sum up what needs to be done from the human side in the process of sanctification—you must *think* and you must *act* (4:8, 9). Thought and practice, mind and body working together, are inseparable. Paul presents these two steps in a highly rhetorical fashion spelling out in considerable detail how a Christian must think and act:

> Think about *these* things:
>> about whatever is truthful,
>> about whatever is majestic,
>> about whatever is just,
>> about whatever is pure,
>> about whatever calls forth love,
>> about whatever is winsome.
> Put into practice *these* things:
>> the lessons you learned from me,
>> and the traditions I passed on to you,
>> and the things you heard from me,
>> and the things you saw in me.

When Paul says "Think about these things" (4:8) he uses a word that means "to reckon, calculate, take into account." It means also "to ponder or let one's mind dwell on." It implies that the Christian is to approach life critically, that is to say, carefully evaluating the worth of the things he allows to govern his life. Fundamentally important to the development of Christians, to their progress toward goodness, is the training of their minds to be able to distinguish between good and bad (cf. Phil 1:9, 10; Heb 5:14), and the consequent rigorous disciplining of themselves so that they will spontaneously choose the good.

Paul knows that what people think about governs their conduct. For this reason he not only encourages Christians to think, but he gives them some idea of the things that they should think about. He says in effect, "Fit yourselves for proper action by filling your minds with proper thoughts." And so he proceeds to make practical suggestions.

1. *Think about things that are true.*

2. *Focus your minds also on things that merit respect.* This phrase, "things that merit respect," is the translation of just one Greek word which is difficult to express in such a way as to include all the ideas contained in it—"things honest, honorable, noble, worthy, venerable," and more. By choosing this word Paul at least means to say that Christians must let their minds be occupied with lofty things, majestic things, things that lift them from the cheap and tawdry to that which is noble and good and of moral worth.

3. *Ponder things that are just;* think about what it means to give to God and people what is due them. This word points to the importance of Christians thinking about duty and obligation and about what they must do to meet their obligations and fulfill them completely.

4. *Think about things that are pure.* By adding this word, "pure," to the list of things to think about the apostle is not asking that the Philippians fix their attention only on those things that foster chastity. He is concerned that they also ponder what is involved in producing purity in motives; he would have them consider that purity of heart which permits a person to see God (cf. Matt 5:8).

5. *Let your minds dwell on all those things that are lovely, amiable, attractive, winsome.* These are the things that, when thought about and put into practice in life, elicit from others not bitterness and hostility, but admiration and affection.

6. Paul ends this list of "good things" to think about, although he makes no pretense that this is an exhaustive list, with a word often translated, *"things of good report"* (KJV). In fact, however, this word has a much more active meaning than that given by the old translation. It conveys also the meaning of "winsome, attractive." It is very similar in idea to the one immediately before it, and thus underscores an important Christian concept: think often and long about those

things that are likely to win people to the faith and will help them grow, rather than let your minds dwell on things that, when practiced, will give offense and drive people away from Christ. As people think, so they act!

These then are the excellent qualities Paul asked the Philippians to focus their minds upon. But it was never his desire that they should merely think about such lofty matters. It was his intent that they should put them into practice. And so he uses still another imperative—"Act! Do!" (v 9).

Paul wants them to put into practice more than just the things he has listed in v 8. Most of these things were but the excellent qualities that belonged to the culture of his day— good ideas borrowed from Greek moral philosophy. Hence what Paul has to say in v 9 follows v 8 and, thus, takes priority. Paul urges the Philippians to go beyond the standards of contemporary culture. They are to put into practice, that is to say, loyally stand by, hold unswervingly to, allow their lives to be controlled by what they heard from him, i.e., be controlled by everything they heard him say that pertains to the gospel of God's saving act in Christ. Furthermore, he wants them to practice what they had seen him do.

What the Philippians had heard from Paul was the gospel—God's power to reconcile people to himself, the dynamic to transform lives and make people over from bad to good and from good to better. This gospel held within itself the energy to send these transformed people out as lights into the darkness, as healers into a sick world, as guideposts for life in the confusion of conflicting ways to travel.

And the things that the Philippians had seen Paul do were things that perfectly coincided with his message. He practiced what he preached. Without arrogance he was able to say, in effect, "I never separated the grand ideas of the Christian gospel from action. I never left them only as high-sounding words and phrases ringing about in people's minds. Rather, I translated them all into deeds. I made it possible for people to see the teachings of the gospel embodied in the way I lived. My conduct made visible and understandable what could have been abstract and elusive ideas. And you must do the same!"

Without embarrassment or hesitation of any sort Paul asserts: "Look! Follow my example! Imitate me!" (Phil 3:17; cf. 1 Cor 11:1). "It is your responsibility as Christians not only to preach the gospel, but to live it."

Fifth, one final step toward sanctification is that Christians are constantly to keep before them Christ as their model. Selfishness is among the most destructive of all sins, if not the most destructive. Its tendency is to push self to the center and God to the periphery of life, and, hence, it borders on idolatry. It sets people against people, destroys unity and cooperation and incites to strife. It makes self-interests primary. It is a fundamental characteristic of this present evil age. Christians, as has been pointed out, while belonging to the new age still bear the marks of the old. It is possible still for selfishness to rise up within them and hinder or destroy their progress toward perfection. How can the Christian combat selfishness and overcome it? Paul's answer: Hold up constantly before your eyes the way of Christ.

In Christ you see one who was in the form of God, in very nature God, who did not consider equality with God something to be used selfishly to his own advantage. Rather, he poured himself out to benefit others; he became a human being and set himself to serve; he humbled himself and did not put himself at the center, but God. He determined to obey God. Hence, God honored and exalted him.

Now, says Paul, this attitude must be your attitude. The same frame of mind toward life that controlled Christ's mind and actions must also control yours. As he set his own self aside and his self-interests and gave first place to the interests of people and God, so you must do the same. And the "should" can become "is," the "ought" can become a reality by steady, constant reflection on this course of action that Christ took, by constantly pondering Christ's conduct, by allowing one's way of thinking to be controlled by the way Christ thought.

Summary

Sanctification, then, includes human effort. There are things that the Christian is expected to do, even required to do. Individual and community responsibility is a theme that pervades Philippians—volition and action, willing the good and doing the good characterize Christians of the new age. But never is this effort thought of as a substitute for or as antecedent to God's saving work in Jesus Christ. The gospel is that people are reconciled to God by the death and resurrection of Christ, by the free gracious gift of life offered them by God, not by anything they can do. No one by dint of human effort can make himself acceptable to God. People can only in humility and awe reach out and take God's free gift (3:3–11).

Nor is the side of sanctification that involves individual or corporate action ever to be thought of as an effort independent of God's continuing gracious prompting and enabling. The Christian life, as formulated by Paul, not only envisions one's own obedience to God's commandments—the human determination to put these commandments into practice. It also envisions an obedience that proceeds from belonging to Christ and from the possession of the Spirit which is at work within the individual Christian and within the church (2:12, 13). These two things must never be thrust apart or viewed separately—God's will does not exclude human volition and action. It includes them, finding its purest fulfillment in their fullest exercise.

7 THE NOTE OF JOY

Of all the themes that can be detected in Philippians, joy is the most obvious. It, too, has great theological significance, for here, as in the Old Testament (cf. Pss 5:11; 9:1, 2; Neh 8:10), joy is ultimately rooted in an unshakeable faith in God and springs from a deep conviction that God acts to save his people.

Three word-groups in the New Testament are translated "joy," "rejoice." The first of these, *agalliaomai/agalliasis*, is used to describe shouts of joy, singing, clapping of hands, lifting up of the voice in glad praise and prayer to God (cf. Luke 1:14, 44, 47). It retains in the New Testament its definite religious sense.

The second word-group, *euphrainō/euphrosynē*, although primarily intended to identify the inner, subjective feelings of merriment and good cheer, also describes the outward expressions of that cheer, such as banqueting, eating, drinking, and making merry (cf. Luke 15:23, 32). These two word-groups are the ones made most use of in the Old Testament. They are, however, used sparingly by the New Testament writers.

The third word-group, *chairō/chara/synchairō*, although originally secular in usage, becomes *the* religious word-group for joy in the New Testament, used a total of 140 times. "Joy" is the hallmark of the Christian era—initiated at the birth of Jesus (Matt 2:10), accented at his resurrection/ascension with the accompanying beginning of the church age (Luke 24:52), and persisting to the present, even when Christians are subjected to suffering (cf. Jas 1:2; 1 Pet 1:6, 7).

Paul never uses words for joy from the first group, and rarely from the second. But the third group is his special word-group. He alone of the New Testament writers accounts for more than fifty uses of such words pertaining to joy. This kind of joy is a distinctive, recurring theme in Paul's letters, in spite of the fact that so much of his own life was marked by pain, disappointments, and afflictions of various kinds (cf. 2 Cor 11:23–30). The words in this group may at one time have been used to describe a mood that stemmed from physical comfort, well-being, and the benefits of health. But these ideas form only a small part of what Paul had in mind when he used them. He usually put these words for joy in contexts of God's saving acts in Christ and the hope for the future that belongs to the Christian because of Christ. Because of this the gospel he preached was a gospel of joy—joy that is not primarily dependent on health, wealth, comfort, or general well-being, but on God.

Joy is a theme that pervades Philippians. Joy here is expressed by the words *chairō* ("to rejoice," nine times—1:18 [twice]; 2:17, 18, 28; 3:1; 4:4 [twice], 10), *chara* ("joy," five times—1:4, 25; 2:2, 29; 4:1) and *synchairō* ("to rejoice with," two times—2:17, 18). To translate these words seems easy enough, but to understand what Paul meant by them is something much more difficult. There appears to be a paradoxical nature to his idea of joy that is not always easy to grasp or express.

On the one hand, joy appears for Paul as that something within a person that is not at all able to be affected by external happenings. For example, Paul was in prison, not as a penalty for crimes done, but as a result of being a witness to Christ (1:13). Yet this unhappy state of affairs did not diminish his joy (1:18).

People, fellow-Christians very likely, treated him with hostility, tried to hurt him, and were set on making his life still more miserable than it already was. Yet this did not affect his joy (1:18).

Even the possibility of his life coming to a violent end could not keep the apostle from being doubly joyful (*chairō* and *synchairō* together in the same sentence—2:17). To quote Barth, joy for Paul was "a defiant 'nevertheless' which [he set] like a full stop against" any resentment, self-pity, anxiety or fear that might otherwise have welled up within him.

Affected by outer circumstance

But on the other hand, joy seems also something that can be affected by external happenings. For example, Paul says that Christians at Philippi were his joy, or the source of his joy, *if they continued to stand firm in the Lord* (4:1). The implication of this conditional expression is that any defection from the faith, any disloyalty to Christ on the part of the Philippians would rob Paul of his joy.

Again, it is clear that the Philippians were capable of increasing Paul's joy by responding positively to his appeal for unity (2:2). Should they fail in this, therefore, their continued disunity would effectively diminish his joy.

Further, Epaphroditus, a person sent by the Philippian church to be Paul's assistant, fell severely ill while serving him. Had he died, had God not had mercy on Paul by sparing Epaphroditus's life, Paul would have had sorrow on top of sorrow—the very opposite of joy (2:27; cf. 2 Cor 2:3). Epa-phroditus's recovery, therefore, was grounds for rejoicing (2:28, 29). Thus joy seems also to be something that can indeed be altered, heightened or diminished, affected in some way by external happenings.

How is the paradox that joy is something unaffected, and yet also affected by external events, to be understood? How is one to reconcile Paul's many remarks about joy and rejoicing which appear again and again in this letter with apparently conflicting meanings?

The resolution of this paradox, and an understanding of what is intended by joy, may come from observing what else Paul wrote about this very important subject. One begins to suspect after careful observation that when he talked of joy he was in reality describing a settled state of mind characterized by what can best be described as peace—an attitude that viewed the world with all of its ups and downs with equanimity, a confident way of looking at life that was rooted in faith, a keen awareness of and trust in the living Lord of the church (1:25, 26). Over and over again Paul reminds himself and the Philippians—and all Christians, for that matter—to "rejoice in the Lord!" (3:1; 4:4, 10).

Hence, for Paul, joy is more than a mood or an emotion, more than a state or feeling, although it includes all these. Joy is rather an understanding of existence that encompasses both elation and depression. It is a world-view that is able to accept with creative submission all events that come along, both of delight and of dismay. It is a perception of reality that generates hope and endurance in affliction and temptation, ease and prosperity, because joy allows one to see beyond any particular event, good or bad, to the sovereign Lord who stands above all events and ultimately has control over them. Joy, to be sure, "includes within itself readiness for martyrdom," but equally the eagerness to go on living and serving, even under the most difficult of circumstances.

NOTES

Introduction
   1. E. Stauffer, *New Testament Theology,* J. Marsh, trans. (London: SCM Press, 1955), 35.

Chapter 2   The Providence of God and the Problem of Evil
   1. J. Jeremias, *New Testament Theology,* J. Bowden, trans. (London: SCM Press, 1971), I. 9.
   2. R. P. Martin, *Philippians,* NCBC (Grand Rapids: Wm. B. Eerdmans, 1980), 84.
   3. J. Macquarrie, *Principles of Christian Theology,* 2nd ed. (New York: Chas. Scribner's Sons, 1977), 219.

Chapter 3   The Person of Christ
   1. K. H. Rengstorf, "Jesus Christ," *NIDNT,* C. Brown, ed. (Grand Rapids: Zondervan, 1976), II. 338.
   2. L. Cerfaux, *Christ in the Theology of Saint Paul* (New York: Herder & Herder, 1959), 501–505.
   3. C. F. D. Moule, *The Origin of Christology* (Cambridge: Cambridge University Press, 1977), 95.
   4. Ibid., 150.
   5. G. Kittel, ed., *TDNT* (Grand Rapids: Wm. B. Eerdmans, 1964), I. 738–40.

Chapter 4 The Christ-Hymn

1. R. Bultmann, *Theology of the New Testament*, K. Grobel, trans. (New York: Chas. Scribner's Sons, 1951), I. 167.

2. J. D. G. Dunn, *Christology in the Making* (Philadelphia: Westminster Press, 1980), 114–21; J. Ziesler, *Pauline Christianity* (New York: Oxford University Press, 1983), 41–44.

3. N. T. Wright, "*Harpagmos* and the Meaning of Philippians ii.5–11," unpublished paper. This paper in revised form has now been published too late for use in this book; see *JTS* 37 (Oct 1986) 321–52.

4. L. Cerfaux, 385.

5. C. F. D. Moule, "The Manhood of Jesus in the New Testament," in *Christ, Faith and History*, S. W. Sykes and J. P. Clayton, eds. (Cambridge: Cambridge University Press, 1976), 97.

6. Wright, see on n. 3.

7. M. Jones, *Philippians* (London: Methenen & Co., 1918), 31, 32.

8. K. Grayston, *The Epistles to the Galatians and to the Philippians* (London: Epworth Press, 1957), *ad loc*.

9. K. Barth, *The Epistle to the Philippians*, J. W. Leitch, trans. (Richmond, Va.: John Knox Press, 1962), 64.

10. Wright, see on n. 3.

11. Ibid.

12. Ibid.

Chapter 6 The Christian Life

1. J. F. Collange, *The Epistle of St. Paul to the Philippians*, A. W. Heathcote, trans. (London: Epworth Press, 1979), 140.

2. J. Ziesler, 85.

3. A. Richardson, *An Introduction to the Theology of the New Testament* (London: SCM Press, 1958), 237.

4. J. J. Müller, *The Epistles of Paul to the Philippians and to Philemon* (Grand Rapids: Wm. B. Eerdmans, 1955), 91.

5. M. Jones, 67. See J. H. Michael, *The Epistle to the Philippians* MNTC (London: Hodder & Stoughton, 1928), 197.

6. K. Barth, 122, 123.

BIBLIOGRAPHY

Barth, K. *The Epistle to the Philippians*. Tr. J. W. Leitch. Richmond, Va.: John Knox Press, 1962.

Beare, F. W. *A Commentary on the Epistle to the Philippians*, BHNTC. London, New York: Harper & Bros., 1959.

Brown:Rengstorf = Rengstorf, K. H., "Jesus Christ," in the *New International Dictionary of New Testament Theology*. Ed. C. Brown. Grand Rapids: Zondervan, 1976, 330–43.

Bultmann, R. *Theology of the New Testament*. Tr. K. Grobel. New York: Chas. Scribner's Sons, 1951, I, 167.

Cerfaux, L. *Christ in the Theology of Saint Paul*. New York: Herder & Herder, 1959, 310.

Collange, J. F. *The Epistle of Saint Paul to the Philippians*. Tr. A. W. Heathcote. London: Epworth Press, 1979.

Dunn, J. D. G. *Christology in the Making*. Philadelphia: Westminster Press, 1980, 114–21.

Grayston, K. *The Epistles to the Galatians and to the Philippians*. London: Epworth Press, 1957.

Hawthorne, G. F. *Philippians*, WBC 43. Waco, Tex.: Word, 1983.

Jeremias, J. *New Testament Theology*. Tr. J. Bowden. London: SCM Press, 1971, I, 9.

Jones, M. *Philippians*. London: Methenen & Co., 1918.

Kittel:Schlier = Schlier, H. *TDNT*. I, Tr. G. W. Bromiley. Grand Rapids: Wm. B. Eerdmans, 1964, 738–40.

Lightfoot, J. B. *Saint Paul's Epistle to the Philippians*. London: Macmillan, 1896.

Macquarrie, J. *Principles of Christian Theology*. 2nd ed. New York: Chas. Scribner's Sons, 1977, 243, 44.

Martin, R. P. *Carmen Christi: Philippians 2:5–11 in Recent Interpretation and in the Setting of Early Christian Worship*. Rev. ed. Grand Rapids: Wm. B. Eerdmans, 1983.

――――. *Philippians*. NCBC, Grand Rapids: Wm. B. Eerdmans, 1980.

MM = Moulton, J. H. and Milligan, G. *The Vocabulary of the Greek New Testament*. Grand Rapids: Wm. B. Eerdmans, 1963.

Moule, C. F. D. "Further Reflexions on Philippians 2:5–11," in *Apostolic History and the Gospel*. Ed. W. W. Gasque and R. P. Martin. Grand Rapids: Wm. B. Eerdmans, 1970.

――――. "The Manhood of Jesus in the New Testament," in *Christ, Faith and History*. Ed. S. W. Sykes and J. P. Clayton. Cambridge: Cambridge University Press, 1976, 95–110.

――――. *The Origin of Christology*. Cambridge: Cambridge University Press, 1977, 95, 126, 150.

Müller, J. J. *The Epistles of Paul to the Philippians and to Philemon*. Grand Rapids: Wm. B. Eerdmans, 1955.

Richardson, A. *An Introduction to the Theology of the New Testament*. London: SCM Press, 1958, 237.

Stauffer, E. *New Testament Theology*. Tr. J. Marsh. London: SCM Press, 1955, 35.

Vincent, M. R. *Critical and Exegetical Commentary on the Epistles to the Philippians and Philemon*. ICC. Edinburgh: T. & T. Clark, 1897.

Wright, N. T., "HARPAGMOS and the Meaning of Philippians ii.5–11," unpublished paper, recently published in a revised form in *JTS* 37 (Oct 1986) 321–52.

Ziesler, J. *Pauline Christianity*. New York: Oxford University Press, 1983, 41–44.

INDEX OF SCRIPTURES

117   *Index of Scriptures*